THE CYCLE
OF
BEAUTY

THE CYCLE
OF BEAUTY

Lectures by

Dharma Master Cheng Yen

English translation by:
Foreign Language Publications Department
English edited by Douglas Shaw

Jing Si Publications Co., Ltd.

"I want to give money to the Master so that she can build hospitals."

"I want to donate money to the Master so she can help people."

Each and every little child who donates his or her piggy bank makes the same wish.

The heart of a child is as pure as a lotus flower.
Our innate nature is also as pure and untainted.
When we are with little children,
we can feel that pure innate nature in them and in us.

When we solicit contributions,
we are also "soliciting" love from people.
See how happy they are as they count the donated money!
But what Master Cheng Yen looks at is not the donations,
but the immeasurable love of children.

This child is doing her part to protect the environment.
Behind her look of concentration is a loving heart.

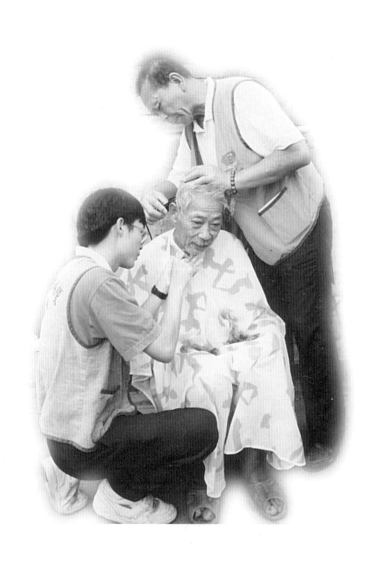

"Please take good care of your heart," the Master tells members of
the Tzu Chi Collegiate Youth Association.
In their hearts seedlings of goodness are growing,
and in their prayers we can see a future of light and hope.

Although these three men were strangers,
they now treat one another like family.
If every one of us can give love even to strangers,
then our world will surely become a very beautiful one.

We must show our love for the earth with our actions,
and not just with words.
The strength of each person is limited,
but when we join our efforts together,
the earth is sure to feel our love.

Senior environmental protection volunteers
smile with deep satisfaction.

After the earthquake of September 21, 1999, the Master paid visits to the disaster areas to spread seeds of Great Love. May the power of love resolve and eliminate all disasters and catastrophes in the world.

After the September 21 earthquake hit Taiwan, the Master kept reminding us to devote ourselves selflessly to the work of relieving suffering and giving joy. We should pass this concept down to the younger generations, so that the spirit of Great Love can be carried on and on.

Translated by Foreign Language Publications Department
English edited by Douglas Shaw
Cover design by Wang Hui-li

Published by Jing Si Publications Co., Ltd.
Foreign Language Publications Department
19, Alley 7, Lane 217, Sec. 3, Zhongxiao East Rd., Taipei, Taiwan
Telephone: 886-2-28989000

Printed May 2005
Third Printing July 2007
ISBN 986-7711-71-8

靜 思 文 化
JING SI PUBLICATIONS
http://www.jingsi.com.tw

TABLE OF CONTENTS

FRAGRANT HEARTS

SELF-ENHANCEMENT

FREE FROM DELUSION AT THE END

Foreword

Birth leads to death, and death initiates life. A new life is normally welcomed and cared for with joy, its arrival symbolic of new hope and development. On the other hand, there are lives that come to the world unwelcome and unblessed, that undergo much misfortune. Buddhist beliefs stress that life originates from the mind and cognition, and it is sustained by causes, circumstances and the power of karma. Life thus comes and goes in an endless cycle of reincarnation according to our karmic conditions, linked by death after birth, birth after death.

What is life?

What is life? Philosophers of all ages, in both the East and West, have made profound inquiries in search of an answer. Asian Confucianism sets life in a positive, secular light. Confucius (551–479 BC) said, "Without knowing life, how is it possible to know death?" Death certainly is inevitable, and it is important for us to learn how to live as decent human beings while we are still alive. Therefore Confucius earnestly advocated the virtues of filial respect towards one's parents, kindness towards one's siblings, benevolence and righteousness. In short, he taught everyone how to be good people. Taoist philosopher Chuang-tzu (c. fourth century BC) said, "Death and birth are but natural occurrences of life, as night and day are regular celestial phenomena." In brief, birth and death are only natural and humans should accept them with composure and ease.

The Greek sage Socrates (470–399 BC) held that the body is merely a requirement for the soul to achieve its objectives and that the soul is the true source of our action. For his student Plato (428–348 BC), the soul is an independent entity that, like ideas, preexists the body and is immortal.

Eastern and Western philosophies have evolved differently from inquiries into the nature of the universe to considerations about man and religion, and they have developed disparate definitions of life and its values. Disregarding these opposing views, the Truth is unchanging.

Buddhism holds that the human body is formed of the Four Elements: earth (which forms the skin, flesh, sinew and bone), water (blood and saliva), fire (bodily warmth), and wind (breath). Life continues only because of the power of karma (the accumulation of an individual's moral actions that exercises influence over the individual in the process of transmigration and life thereafter). The *Sutra of Profound Gratitude to Parents* chronicles an incident that took place when the Buddha led the sangha (the assembly of monks and nuns) on a journey. On seeing a pile of bones by the roadside, the Buddha reverently knelt and touched the ground with his forehead. Then he explained to the perplexed Ananda, his disciple and attendant, "These bones belonged to my ancestors in my previous life and to my parents in many of my other lives. For this tie formed in the past, I revere them today."

It can be understood from the Buddha's words that he had come to and left the human world countless times, and that life does not cease to exist after the aging and death of one lifetime, but is carried on perpetually in the wheel of reincarnation. Life springs from the combination of all causes and conditions, just as all things on earth ebb and flow with the drift of life and the four seasons rotate unceasingly, silently teaching the dharma (the Buddha's teachings on the true nature of the universe).

The truth about the world

In the *Sutra of the Bodhisattvas' Eight Realizations*, the First Realization is:

The world is impermanent, and the land is fragile.
The Four Elements are suffering and emptiness, and the Five Aggregates are not "I."
Birth, death, transformation and change are all unreal, illusory phenomena beyond our control.
Our hearts are the origin of all evil, and our bodies are the reservoir of all sin.
If we can observe all this, we will gradually become free from life and death.

This clearly points out that the four phases of the world— formation, existence, destruction and void—are impermanent and that the heart is the fountainhead of all we do. Master Cheng Yen once spoke about the impermanence of life: "When the Four Elements exist in moderation and harmony, peace is attained; if not, disasters arise. For example, excessive movement of the earth causes earthquakes, immoderate wind gives rise to typhoons, and inordinate fire occasions droughts. Human interference today, such as air and soil pollution, has caused even more disruption of the elements."

In our modern times, industrialization and technological advances have vastly enhanced the material life of mankind, but have not produced satisfaction of the mind. In the incessant pursuit to satiate their desires, people have allowed their

souls to grow hollow. Human over-development has adverse-
ly influenced, both directly and indirectly, the earth's environment and ecosystems, as manifested in the gradual worsening
of the El Niño and La Niña climatic phenomena.

In 1998, Afghanistan was shaken by a massive earthquake
while hurricanes left Central and South America in tatters. The
following year, the world saw the genocide in Kosovo and the
devastating earthquakes in Turkey. Natural and man-made
disasters caused catastrophic losses in countless innocent lives
and homes. Even our homeland, Taiwan, has suffered disasters
such as floods and mudslides induced by typhoons, the China
Airlines plane crash, and the earthquake of September 21, 1999,
that was of a magnitude not seen in almost a century. All these
events arouse apprehension and make one wonder: when will
Mother Nature rest from her counterattacks? When will the
tragedies in the world ever end?

Traditional values are on the wane in our society, which has
become infested with disorder and crime. In the Chinese classic
Book of Rites, "The Commonwealth State" is so described:

*Therefore people will respect all the elderly as though they
were their own parents, and love all the young as though they
were their own children. The elderly will have decent homes in
which to pass their days; adults will be able to make use of
their abilities; the young will be nurtured properly. Means of
support will be provided for widowers, widows, orphans, the
childless, disabled and sick. Each man and woman will have a
proper role to play. One will be sorry to see goods wasted
while not necessarily wanting to possess them. One will
regret that efforts are not made by oneself while not necessarily wanting the rewards from those efforts to serve oneself.*

Regrettably, such ethical values have gradually been erod-
ed by the modern fast-food culture.

What exactly has gone wrong in our society? How is it that
the young no longer want to stay at home and are apathetic
toward their parents? Then there are the elderly, who have
become a group tucked away in a corner of society, often
neglected. In fact, family ethics represent the most ingenuous,
pristine love of humanity and form the cornerstone of society.
When family ethics are weakened, both family and society
will suffer from disorder. Restoring our former moral principles and values is at present our most pressing task.

The twentieth century's most famous educator-philoso-
pher, Dr. John Dewey (1859–1952), thought that humans are
born with the natures of "differentiation" and "integration,"
respectively producing selfish and altruistic drives. The stability and development of society depend on the coordination
and balance of these two forces. Master Cheng Yen also made
a similar observation: "When the interaction of goodness and
power of love exist between people, then society will certainly be harmonious and full of warmth. Whether there are
blessings or disasters in the world is determined by the
human heart, which can lean toward either good or evil. Only
if everyone embarks on the road of goodness and charity will
there be peace and happiness in the world."

Facing life and death with a positive attitude

In the first section of this book, *Fragrant Hearts*, there is a
story of a child who saves coins in a piggy bank every day to
help Master Cheng Yen construct hospitals. In that young
heart there is love that will continue into adulthood, growing

ever more abundant. Members of the Tzu Chi Collegiate Youth Association volunteer at hospitals to serve patients, whereby they learn the meaning and value of life and are prompted to more actively employ their abilities and purify their hearts. Many other kindhearted people also silently contribute their efforts to society. All these people are like lotuses that grow from the muck and mire, untainted by the polluted environment and emanating a fragrance that makes the world a better place.

The Buddha taught, "There is no difference between the mind, the Buddha, and all living beings." Everyone has the buddha-nature, but the mind is also the source of confusion and evil actions that create bad karma. According to the *Surangama Sutra*: "All beings have existed in the cycle of life and death since time immemorial. This is because they do not see their true self that eternally abides within, their pure nature and their clear perception. They are preoccupied by false delusions and therefore remain in the endless cycle of reincarnation." Rediscovering our pure nature and returning to our original self are endeavors that require earnest cultivation.

In the second section of this book, *Self-Enhancement*, there is a story of an old man who asks the Buddha for a way to eliminate sickness. The Buddha replies that when physical sickness does not affect one's psychology, then one can be emancipated from the pain. All living beings suffer from anxieties arising from the Five Aggregates (form, sensation, perception, impulse and consciousness). Once one is taken ill, life is further enshrouded in the fear of pain and death. If one could fully understand that the body really has no form and let aging, sickness and death run their natural courses, then physical suffering will naturally become less intense and unbearable. Master Cheng Yen once said, "Let go of any physical or psychological attachments and fulfill your daily duties, then you will realize the true value of your life." One who knows the Truth will not be deluded or disoriented, but will have a crystal-clear heart unfettered by ignorance and anxiety.

A Buddhist sutra states, "Life exists between breaths." The world we reside in is referred to as the "world of endurance of suffering," because there is no peace in the Three Realms of human existence (the realms of sensuous desire, of form, and of the formless realm of pure spirit), where pain far exceeds happiness. In the Three Realms, what happiness we do enjoy is based upon fleeting illusory circumstances that result in endless suffering when they cease. The great thinker, Arthur Schopenhauer (1788–1860), believed that the process of human life is a chronicle of pain, because there is no end to desire and any satisfaction is only temporary. Master Cheng Yen once said, "You do not have the right to own your life, only the right to use it." Given that the body is only a phenomenal combination of the Four Elements, the only way to make it meaningful is to employ its capacity to the fullest. Then one will remain joyful and at ease even when one reaches the final stop in life.

The ancient Chinese historian Ssu-ma Chien (145–90 BC) believed, "Everyone encounters death, which can be as weighty as Mount Tai or as light as a feather—the difference lies in what purpose one's death serves." Death is the inescapable route of every human being, but the Chinese, fearing death and considering any discussion of it unlucky, tend to avoid the subject. Therefore, once nearing that final end, many people, old and young alike, feel lost and fearful because they do not know what comes after. All major world religions, such as Christianity, Buddhism, Islam, Hinduism and Judaism, teach believers to face death with a positive attitude. How does Buddhism guide the dying to face the end with a peaceful and calm attitude? Master Hung Yi once taught, "Although the dying person is aided by the chanting of the holy name of the Amitabha Buddha and appropriate rituals, a tranquil, unencumbered death is enabled only by self-cultivation and preparation in normal times." Master Cheng Yen taught us to see the truth about life and death: "Life continues in an endless circle powered by karma. The essential thing is to eliminate anxiety. If that is not accomplished, reincarnation will never end."

In the third and final section of this book, *Free from Delusion at the End*, real-life examples demonstrate that as long as one knows how to let go, one can transcend worries about life and death. One example is a terminal cancer patient who rejects chemotherapy in order to preserve his body for future medical research. Other instances are old people who serenely end their life's journey.

"Life is hard and impermanent," Master Cheng Yen said. "Fortunately, there is a group of incarnate bodhisattvas who lovingly devote themselves to the work of relieving suffering and giving joy, not only in Taiwan but around the world. Everything in life begins with the mind. The work of purifying one's mind, cultivating oneself and helping others resembles that of climbing a high mountain: although the path is rugged, if one persistently advances by taking one step at a time, the goal can be achieved."

In our brief lives, how do we leave legacies that we will not regret? It depends entirely on how we see life and whether we respect life and use our innate abilities wisely. Ultimately, we must bring no shame to our family and ourselves.

Fragrant Hearts

Our pure innate nature emits a wonderful fragrance, pacifying our agitated minds, eliminating our worldly worries, and cleansing the muddy waters of our hearts. Eventually it will allow us to see our pure selves.

A Story of a Young Bodhisattva

We must live in harmony with the motion of the universe. Human beings go through the stages of birth, aging, illness and death, just like the seasonal changes of spring, summer, autumn and winter in nature. There is a close connection between the two. Birth, aging, illness and death are what all of us have to experience, but do we know what exactly "death" is? Actually, it is simply the termination of life, not the soul. Our consciousness will drift with our karma and change its form after we breathe our last breath. Our innate nature remains alive and, like the seasonal changes, goes on in an endless cycle.

Buddhists believe in reincarnation. Someone once asked me, "When we die, that's the end of us. How do we know we will be reborn?" Let's try to find the answer. Not only do Buddhist scriptures contain the concept of reincarnation, but many Buddhist masters in the past also put a great deal of emphasis on this idea. Besides Buddhism, other religions also talk about the concept of the soul.

There is a belief in Catholicism, for instance, that those who believe in God will ascend to heaven. Catholics believe that when the body perishes the soul will ascend to heaven or descend to hell, while Buddhists hold that those who do good deeds will be happier in the next life and those who do bad deeds will suffer. What we do every day will become our karma. There is a saying: "Nothing but our karma follows us when we die." If we vow to do good things for the world, we will return to the earth as good human beings; if we die with evil thoughts, we will be bogged down by bad karma after we are reborn.

There are those who wonder if people really return to this world after they die. From my past experiences, I think the answer is yes. I have seen many babies who cannot yet talk, but are so happy to hear the words "Tzu Chi" and are so respectful towards me. Since one's behavior arises from one's subconscious, they must have been Tzu Chi people before and the seeds of goodness must be deeply rooted in their nature.

Once when I went to Taipei, an elderly commissioner brought her daughter-in-law and her little granddaughter to see me. The child was around two years old. She bounced into the room carrying a heavy object, which she had to put on the floor because of its weight.

Standing in front of me, she folded her hands together and then prostrated herself like Buddhists do when seeing their dharma master. "One prostration is enough," I told her. But she prostrated herself two more times [which is the proper greeting to dharma masters]. Then with all her strength she lifted up the heavy piggy bank and staggered towards me. I asked her, "What is this for?" She replied, "I'd like to give you this to build hospitals." I took the piggy bank from her, and it certainly was heavy!

After all the coins were taken out of the piggy bank, she took it back and then asked for five dollars from her mother. Her mother asked her, "What do you want the money for?" She replied, "For the Master to build hospitals." Her mother fished out some coins from her pocket and handed them to her.

Just as the little girl was about to put all the coins into the piggy bank, a commissioner held her hand and took the coins away. "Let's go buy some candy," she said. The little girl immediately took back the money, dropped it all into the piggy bank, and said, "These are for the Master to build hospitals!" Someone took away the piggy bank and teased her, "The money is for you to buy candy!" She snatched it back, pouted, and said, "This is for the Master to build hospitals!" She stared angrily at the adults.

"My granddaughter is very special," her grandmother said. "She often asks for five dollars from me and says that she wants to help the Master build a hospital." Every morning when she came home from grocery shopping, her granddaughter, hearing her opening the door, would run to the door and ask her for five dollars.

After hearing this story, I took a look at the girl. She never forgot about saving money for me to construct hospitals! It reminded me how Tzu Chi started with fifty cents—our commissioners saved fifty cents in their bamboo "piggy banks" every day to be used for charity. The hardships these early commissioners endured when they were raising money for the construction of the Tzu Chi Hospital in Hualien was imprinted on their minds. Maybe this little girl was the reincarnation of one of those early commissioners.

When the girl was only one year old, she saw a photograph of me in the living room. She pointed at it, and her grandmother told her, "That's Master Cheng Yen." Thereupon the girl put her palms together and prostrated herself before the photo. Since then, whenever she saw the photo, she would fold her hands and say, "Master," and then prostrate herself before the photo. This toddler must be spiritually connected to me. Otherwise, why would a one-year-old girl show so much respect for me? And why would she always think of building hospitals when she heard the clink of coins?

It is evident from the above example that our innate nature is everlasting and that it comes and goes through the cycle of reincarnation, driven by our karma. Therefore, if we want to be happy in our next life, we must vow to do good deeds and create good karma. Only by continually doing good deeds can we keep ourselves from creating bad karma and suffering in our next life.

A Fresh New Life

We hear birds singing in harmony every morning at the Abode of Still Thoughts [the residence of Master Cheng Yen and her disciples, and the headquarters of the Tzu Chi Foundation]. They chirp away with such energy and vigor as they welcome the new day! We should try to live a fresh, new life each day like the birds. As long as we keep our hearts fresh and clear, every day can be a new beginning for us.

We are all born with a good human nature that is most clearly manifested in little children. In Tzu Chi, we have a Children's Achievement Class. Once I went to Taichung, and a Professor Tseng showed me several compositions written by children who attended the class. Their compositions filled me with happiness and showed that our future was full of hope.

A child who was in first or second grade wrote down three wishes: "My first wish is that no one in the world will fall sick; my second wish is that Master Cheng Yen will pay us more visits; and my third wish is that I will be among the top ten of my class." What wonderful wishes he made!

First he wished that no one would suffer from illness. How kind-hearted the child was! From seeing other people fall ill he realized that sickness brings a lot of suffering, so even though he was still very young he felt pity towards those who were ill. His second wish was that I could go visit them more often. This wish reflects his aspiration to meet with someone he loves. His third wish was to be diligent. He made a wish to study hard and to be among the top ten of his class. Look! Even such a little child knows to aspire towards self-improvement.

In the Achievement Class, volunteer mothers designed an activity which aimed to help children understand the inconveniences facing handicapped people and learn to appreciate what they had. They blindfolded the children and told them to practice walking as if they were blind. The children also learned how to put on clothes and paint by holding brushes in their mouths, like people who have no hands must do. After these classes, the children all deeply realized how wonderful it is to have eyes and hands.

The volunteer mothers also asked the students to draw a picture on paper on which a circle, a square and an oval had already been drawn and to give it a title. One drew a smiling face and wrote, "The most beautiful face is a smiling face." The same child drew a lot of rice plants in the square and wrote, "Cultivate your field of blessings." In the oval he drew three leaves and a dot in the center. "The mind creates all," he explained. What a wonderful imagination!

The teachers of the Children's Achievement Class do a good job too. They advise their students to apply what they learn from my book, *Still Thoughts*, to their daily lives and thereby influence their families. With their minds purified every day, the children live lives full of goodness. They know how to cherish their lives. Their world is indeed full of hope!

Children are like blank sheets of paper, taking on whatever the adults teach them. They have the most unsophisticated hearts. The Buddha taught us that we should have the heart of a child, the patience of a camel, and the courage of a lion. Acquiring these qualities should be the goal of our lives. No matter how hard it is to reach this goal, as long as we persevere we will make it.

Look for the Goodness in People

One day a group of children came to see me. One rather dignified little girl prostrated herself before me.

"Are you a student from the Children's Achievement Class?" I asked her.

"Yes, I am."

"Which class do you attend?"

"I'm in the Confidence Class."

"Is that the one for the youngest children?"

"Yes," she replied with a clear, childish voice.

"What have you learned in your class?"

She pondered for a moment and then said, "I learned how to compliment other people."

"Really? Then, now that you've seen me, would you like to compliment me?"

She stood thinking for a brief moment and then said to me, "Master, you are a most loving and compassionate person!" Such a sweet girl! And she was only seven years old!

"You're a good, lovely girl," I commended her. She beamed with joy when she heard that. Right at that moment, a little boy who was also only seven years old walked into the room. I spoke to him: "Are you also attending the Confidence Class? Have you learned anything from the class?"

He walked up to me and replied, "Yes."

"This little girl is very lovely. She knows how to compliment people. Do you know how to compliment people too?"

He turned to look at her and said, "I can't see anything good in her."

"How can you say something like that? She knows how to compliment other people, so she is an adorable girl. Come, take one more look at her and tell me how good she is."

But he stubbornly refused to do so. "There's nothing good about her."

"Come, look at him," I said to the girl. "Would you like to praise him?"

"I can't see anything good in him either," she said.

"That's not right," I said to her. "Didn't you just say that you had learned to compliment other people? Come, don't focus on his shortcomings; just tell me his good points."

She looked at him innocently and then said, "Hmm, he's dressed very neatly today. He's cute."

I turned to the boy. "See? She praised your appearance! Come, take a look at her and tell me what's good about her."

He looked at her and said, "Hmm, she's cute because she compliments other people."

I smiled. "Good children, you two know how to compliment each other. Let me give you a reward." I gave each one of them a piece of candy, which made them very happy.

Look at the world of children—how innocent they are! At first the two children were outspoken and said straight out what they thought of each other. But when I asked them to find the good points in each other, they did what I told them to do. Can we adults be like them? It must be difficult. Grown-ups tend to focus on other people's shortcomings instead of their merits.

People enjoy finding fault with others, but finding fault is a fault. We should be open-minded so that we can see the best in people. If we spend our days finding fault with each other, our lives will be full of faults. It is a pity to live a "faulty life" like this. Human beings are so bogged down with faults that their lives become difficult for them. If we want our lives to go right, we should pay more attention to other people's merits instead of their shortcomings.

We must examine ourselves regularly to see if we have any weaknesses. Other people may belittle us, but if we stay unruffled and look earnestly for their good points instead of taking offense, then it will not be hard for us to forgive and even admire them. When other people see our response, they will also calm down and see some good in us.

Take these two little children for example. The little girl was good at complimenting other people, but when the boy came in, he ruined the atmosphere by refusing to say any good words. When I asked the girl to look for the good points in the boy, she pondered for a few moments and then said that he was nicely dressed and looked cute. Her words lightened the atmosphere. When the boy looked at the girl again, he also complimented her for being kind and cute. We adults should learn to be like them.

In life, adversities are inevitable. Adversities are opportunities for us to adjust our attitudes and to reflect on ourselves. We are likely to remain oblivious to our shortcomings if nothing induces us to look into ourselves. Thus, we must be thankful for the difficulties that come our way because they remind us to reflect on ourselves.

On the road of life, we must try to discover and concentrate on other people's merits. If we can do this, we will collect merits and become better persons. As long as we focus on the goodness of life, the road ahead of us will be even and smooth.

Sincere Love

The hearts of children are naïve, innocent and kind because they have innate wisdom. As we grow up, we accumulate worldly knowledge from our interactions with the world and other people. Although the environment may affect the way we look at the world, our innate wisdom is always there.

During one Chinese New Year holiday, a lovely child who was only two years old came to see me. "Happy New Year, Master," he greeted me. I gave him a piece of candy in return for his greetings, and he happily ran off with it. But a while later he came back again with the same piece of candy and handed it back to me. "Please take this, Master."

"Why? I just gave it to you."

"I can't eat it. My teeth will go bad!"

Suddenly I remembered that he liked peanuts, so I asked him, "Will peanuts hurt your teeth?" He thought it over for a while and then replied, "No, they won't." The more peanuts, the better—he opened his two front pockets for me to fill with peanuts. This little event showed that even a little child has knowledge, which in this case he had acquired from adults: "Don't eat too much candy or you will get cavities." However, his innocence returned when he saw the peanuts. He went ahead and took what he wanted.

There is another type of sincere love in Tzu Chi—giving without asking for anything in return. Most people try to avoid the sick, but the unselfishness of Tzu Chi people enables them to take care of sick people with love and care. When they visit lonely old people, they are not concerned about their filthy, impoverished environments. Because of their sincerity, they unflinchingly proceed on the path of helping the needy.

It is hard for people to maintain that sincere love, so I am very happy that children growing up in the Tzu Chi world all have sincere hearts. Whenever they get some money, their first thought is to give it to me to build hospitals. I often ask them, "Why don't you keep it and get something for yourself?" They always answer, "I feel more at ease when I give it to you."

Three children once came from Kaohsiung to see me. Before they left, they came into my study to say goodbye to me. The oldest brother said, "Master, I'll come to see you again when I have time." The younger brother said, "I'll keep on saving money for you to build hospitals." If they can stay so kind-hearted, there is little chance that they will become bad people.

Children are all so adorable. At the beginning of this year, a young girl and her three brothers came to see me. Their grandmother and uncles who lived in the United States had sent them red envelopes of money [traditional Chinese New Year presents] that contained US dollars. When these children came to see me, each of them gave me a box of candy and a red envelope.

"Are you returning the red envelopes I gave you?" I teased them.

The young girl replied, "No, we're giving you more than what you gave us yesterday." I took the money out of the red envelope, and saw that there were two US$100 bills in it. I said to her, "Wow, that's a lot of money!" She said, "Yes, I got it from my uncle in the States, and now I'm giving it to you, Master, to build hospitals."

Her brothers each gave me the same amount of money. I asked the youngest one, "Since you're the youngest in your family, are you going to give less money?"

He said, "No, I'm giving you more than my sister and my brothers gave you." He happily took out a big piggy bank and placed it before me.

When that youngest brother first came to Tzu Chi, he was only three. Since then, he has been saving money for me to build hospitals. A three-year-old doesn't know how to spend money, so he just put whatever he got into his piggy bank. He is now about to enter junior high school, and he still feeds his piggy bank regularly.

It is essential to instill love into children's minds when they are still young. Whenever I see them, I feel that our future is full of hope. I believe our society will become a better place when they grow up.

Mature beyond His Years

We are all born with an innate buddha-nature, also known as our life of wisdom. This innate nature houses undefiled wisdom and compassion, so all of us, regardless of our age, possess intrinsic love.

Once when I was in the Tzu Chi office in Taipei, a lot of lovely children came to see me. One fifth grader came with his mother. He brought with him a big piggy bank which was so heavy that his mother had to carry it for him. He handed the piggy bank to me respectfully.

"What is this for?" I asked him.

"This is for you to build hospitals and schools and to relieve people from suffering," he said. "I will make money and donate it to Tzu Chi, and then I will become an Honorary Board member [a patron who has donated over NT$1 million, or about US$31,000]." His mother smiled and said, "This child has wanted to become an Honorary Board member since he was in second grade."

One day when the child was in second grade, he attended a Tzu Chi certification ceremony. He knew that the ceremony was not to certify new commissioners, so he asked his mother who these people were. She replied, "They are Honorary Board members who donate money to help the Master build hospitals and schools and relieve people of suffering."

Although he was still a little child, his intrinsic love had been activated. From that time on, he vowed to become an Honorary Board member who would do good deeds and help people in distress.

When his father learned of the boy's vow, he said to him, "If you are a good boy, I'll donate money in your name and make your wish come true."

"No, I want to donate my own money," he answered.

"How can you possibly get so much money?"

"I'll be a good boy, and then I'll make money."

"How?"

"Many kids study hard and get good grades," the boy replied seriously, "and their parents reward them by giving them money."

In order to encourage him, his father said, "Sure! If you study hard and behave yourself, I'll do the same."

"Some of my friends also earn money by doing chores for their mothers," the boy added.

"OK, if you help me do the dishes and sweep the floor, I'll give you an allowance."

After that, the boy always put his pocket money into his piggy bank.

This child was mature beyond his years. He knew the importance of helping the world, so he made a good commitment which he had been keeping for the past three years. His behavior bears witness to what I call undefiled love. Love is very powerful, and how great one's love is depends not on one's age or background, but on whether one has a pure, loving heart.

Nowadays many people consider the moral degeneration of the world to be worsening every day. The truth is that many people of different ages, such as Tzu Chi people, are still silently and determinedly doing good deeds. I sincerely believe in what the Buddha said: "Whether one has wisdom or not does not depend on one's age." The life of wisdom is pure and everlasting. I hope to spread love between people so that everyone knows how to respect and love each other.

Take overseas members of the Tzu Chi Collegiate Youth Association as an example. Most people at that age are looking for fun, but these youngsters return to Taiwan whenever they are on holiday to learn more about the Tzu Chi spirit. When I was at the Tzu Chi branch office in Taichung in the winter of 1998, there was a Youth Association training seminar. I was very grateful to the commissioners who lived there. They cared for these young people lovingly and made them feel at home. Because of this abundant love, the young people fully enjoyed themselves and learned a great deal during the training courses.

Later these young people came to the Abode of Still Thoughts, the spiritual home of Tzu Chi members. There they nurtured the seeds of love in them and learned to spread the seeds abroad. To create a network of love, they worked enthusiastically to set up an organizational framework for overseas members of the Tzu Chi Collegiate Youth Association.

I often say, "Come cultivate the field of blessings and together create a Tzu Chi world with unlimited compassion and love." We all know that as we sow, so shall we reap. Every Youth Association member is like a lotus blossom of love. One day these flowers will be in full bloom, sending out the fragrance of love to every corner of the world. Our world will surely become a purer and more wonderful place to live in. When we all give unselfishly and combine our efforts to spread love, better times will await us.

Sunlight That Warms the Heart

The road of life seems rough and hard to walk on. Why? It is because fellow travelers do not join hands, are not of one heart, and don't love or respect each other. Therefore, confrontations and conflicts abound in our society. How it worries one!

But when we look at the Tzu Chi world, we feel hope and peace. During summer vacations, many teachers and college students come to the Hualien Tzu Chi Hospital to work as volunteers. With love in their hearts, they all want to help others.

Our Tzu Chi TV station once reported on a group of overseas Tzu Chi Collegiate Youth Association members, both undergraduate and graduate students, who came from many different countries. These young people were not only smart—they were also loving and caring. They loved Tzu Chi and Taiwan, so they always hurried back to Taiwan as soon as summer vacation arrived. They returned to their home country with only one goal in mind: to be Tzu Chi volunteers. They wanted to learn about Tzu Chi's Great Love, and they wanted to dedicate their love to those who were in need of help.

For several weeks, they cared for patients in the hospital, hoping to alleviate their psychological and physical pain. They sang and danced to entertain patients, and they tenderly massaged old patients and listened to their stories.

Some of the elderly people felt upset because their children and grandchildren didn't come to visit them. "Don't be sad about that," one student volunteer comforted an elderly patient. "They're probably too busy. You can treat me as your grandchild. I'll call you 'Grandpa,' so I'll be like your grandson!"

The students brought joy not only to the patients but also to themselves. Through their experiences of caring for others, they learned to appreciate what they had. Before, they didn't feel that they were fortunate or that their parents loved them, nor did they feel the need to give anything back to their parents. But after what they saw in the hospital—worried parents carefully attending to their children—they came to realize how much their parents loved them.

They also noticed the loneliness of the elderly patients in the hospital, and they felt sorry for them because no one cared for them when they fell ill. Seeing their situation, the young people felt that the children of these elderly patients were behaving in a very unworthy way. How could they turn a blind eye to their parents when they were most in need of their care? They reflected on the situation and vowed that when their own parents get old and sick, they would never allow them to be left unattended.

In addition to helping out in the hospital, these young people also paid visits to former patients who had been discharged from the hospital. Our hospital regularly follows up on patients, especially those who are old, poor or whose families have problems. Students who volunteer in our hospital often accompany our regular volunteers on these home-care visits.

Many touching stories happen during the process. One patient under our care was an eccentric and unsociable old veteran. He had the idea that people who were good to him were only being condescending to him, and he gradually became secluded from the world. But when he came to our hospital for treatment, our volunteers took good care of him and talked to him. Their sincerity and kindness touched him and he was finally willing to open himself up.

When the doctor told him that he was well enough to leave the hospital, he refused to go. He loved it there, because so many people there cared about him. Our volunteers had to persuade him that since he had recovered from his illness, he should go home to recuperate. Nevertheless, he was afraid that once he left the hospital he would be separated from the volunteers, and he couldn't bear to part with them. When the volunteers promised him that they would go visit him often, the old man finally agreed to go home.

Thereafter, the hospital volunteers often brought young people to visit the old veteran. He was an industrious man. He built the walls around his house himself with stones he had collected. He also planted and grew vegetables in the patches of garden in front of and behind his home.

The young people the volunteers brought along to the old man's house were very kind. Once while helping him with his bath, they picked up a washcloth to scrub the old man's back. A volunteer saw this and asked the old man, "Grandpa, do you have a cleaner washcloth?

"Sure, I have five."

"How come this one's so dirty?"

"Oh, because that's a dishcloth." Embarrassed, the young people went to fetch another bucket of water and washed him again.

The interaction between the volunteers and the old man opened his heart. Their love was like sunlight shining into his heart and making him feel the warmth of society. The chance to serve the old man also inspired the young people to be more grateful. When the veteran said, "I'm old and useless," they would respond, "Who says so? When you were young you fought for our country, so now we can live comfortably. We should be especially grateful to you."

Sick and alone, the old veteran used to feel forlorn. But these young people opened his heart and made him realize that even though he had no family in the world, there were still people who cared for him. These young people made the best of their time and abilities to take care of elderly, sick people. They not only comforted lonely old people, but also gained a lot of precious experiences from serving them. Isn't the energy of these young people like the radiant warmth of the morning sun?

A Sense of Mission

We sometimes hear people say, "Why are you putting me down?" I wonder why people are so afraid that others are looking down on them. It must be because they are too self-conscious. Why are others unsatisfied with you? It is because you inflate your ego too much, and your egotism makes it hard for other people to look up to and accept you. When you and others fail to accept each other, a lot of pain will ensue.

In Tzu Chi we learn how to live our lives. How do we lead a happy life? First we must learn to be decent human beings by learning to love people. If you love others, they will love you too. If you don't know how to get along with people, then you don't know how to be a decent human being.

In addition, we must learn how to do things properly. We should earnestly do the things that we ought to do without asking for repayment. At the same time, we should restrain ourselves from doing improper things. Buddhism emphasizes discipline, because it can forestall mistakes. However, if we accidentally make a mistake, we must correct it right away.

If we stay constantly alert and know how to do the right things, we will have no regrets in our lives. "The greatest punishment in life is regret." To regret our mistakes is painful, so we must know how to tell right from wrong and hold onto what is right. Furthermore, we must also know that learning is a never-ending process, and that the ability to choose the right things to learn is also a kind of wisdom.

In addition, we must try to be sociable. No one can live alone, for we all must rely on each other in order to live. Nothing in life can be done single-handedly without the help of others. For example, the roads we walk or drive on were paved by others and the houses we live in were built with the hard work of laborers. Since we depend on people in different walks of life to provide us with food, clothes, shelter and transportation, we must be grateful for all the things that we receive and repay our society, to which we owe so much. If all of us can get along with others harmoniously and lovingly and devote ourselves to our society, then we will be living a truly valuable, blissful and happy life.

In today's society, people put a lot of emphasis on diplomas. One year Dr. Lee Yuan-tseh, president of Academia Sinica, was invited to speak at the graduation ceremony of the Tzu Chi College of Medicine. He began his speech to our graduating class by saying, "Dear students, do not depend solely on your diploma to give you a good future. Remember, a diploma doesn't stand for everything you are."

No doubt, a diploma is not equivalent to a person's value and your professional knowledge may not be useful to you all your life. Those who study medicine don't necessarily become doctors after they graduate, and those who major in economics don't always work in business. Many people get better, more suitable jobs after they graduate. Furthermore, all of us will retire one day, so our vocational knowledge won't follow us all our life.

What will stay with us is our knowledge of life and the humanities. To learn such knowledge we should ask ourselves the following: Do we pay enough attention to the people and events in our everyday life? Does our wisdom grow with our age? Are we striving to maintain harmony with our family and with colleagues? To live meaningfully, we must have worthy goals in life and always work toward them. Therefore, such lessons of life are indispensable.

We all come to this world with a mission. But some people don't know how to live their lives and they become disoriented, so much so that they sometimes hurt themselves and disturb society. I consider the most important thing in life to be: Be a good person and cooperate with others. If each of us can respect and appreciate each other, a beautiful and good society will naturally form.

Senior Environmental Protection Bodhisattvas

Heavy rainfall-induced disasters seem to be on the rise in the world today. In Taiwan even a moderate rain frequently leads to mudslides and floods, phenomena seldom seen in the past. I believe the main reason is because people have paid little attention to water and soil conservation. To save the island, environmental protection is a task that cannot be delayed.

Some time ago, Tzu Chi environmental protection volunteers from all over the island came to the Abode of Still Thoughts to attend a seminar on environmental protection. Many people tend to think that environmental protection consists only of recycling and separating garbage, but actually there is more to it than that. Why should we protect our environment? How essential is environmental protection to the earth? In order to have a deeper understanding of the issues, it was important for the environmental protection volunteers to attend this seminar.

A senior volunteer once shared with us her experiences in protecting the environment. Her story was really touching. "The earth is ours," she kept telling us, "and it is our responsibility to take good care of it." She thought that Tzu Chi needed more capable people to pitch in, and through its environmental protection work it could draw and cultivate more talent. She said that the foundation had done a lot for our society and she cited herself as an example. She was only an environmental protection volunteer, but because of her hard work she had motivated many of her neighbors—some of them were business managers and some housewives—to join Tzu Chi. Now seven of them have become trainee commissioners.

"I'm very old now," she said humbly, "and I'm not sure how much more I can do." Actually, as long as we are diligent and sincere and continue to help others, we will be able to attract more people to join us. This old lady once broke six ribs in a car accident. If the same thing happened to other people, they might think, "I'm always doing good deeds. How can something like this happen to me? It's just my bad luck that I was the only person injured in the car." However, she thought otherwise: "Thank the Buddha that I'm okay. Only my ribs were injured and now I'm fine. I'm really lucky."

Her only worry was that the injury might prevent her from doing environmental protection work in the future. But a neighbor encouraged her: "You can just sit and tell us what to do. Don't move any heavy objects."

"Yes, she's right," she thought. "This way I can still be useful." She felt relieved after knowing that she could still be of some use, and consequently she recovered rapidly. Now she is often seen calling out to her neighbors as they sort out garbage: "Come have some snacks." "Please help move this." "Okay, it's time to take a rest." What a kind old bodhisattva she is!

In the seminar, several other elderly environmental protection volunteers also came up to the stage to share their experiences. Their speeches were all very interesting. A volunteer from eastern Taiwan told us, "Actually, I didn't even make it through elementary school. When people ask me what I can do, I tell them I know how to recycle garbage. Now I even joke that I graduated from National Taiwan University with a major in garbage recycling. We all grew up in Taiwan, and of course we should cherish our homeland."

That volunteer was right. Society is like a big university in which we can live and learn until we reach an old age. Our hearts will remain forever young this way.

Someone once said that it's truly valuable to be a student of "Tzu Chi University." Now, all of us are classmates. We have to love our environment and we have to be nice and helpful to everyone. After we graduate from Tzu Chi, we should continue to walk on the Path of the Bodhisattvas. The path from being mediocre, ordinary people to becoming bodhisattvas is sacred and full of trials. So let's all work hard.

Marching in a Circle

For more than one week every month, I tour around the island visiting Tzu Chi offices. During those ten-odd days, everything I see or hear manifests love. This time my first stop was in Ilan. One commissioner there told me that last December they all worked long hours, from early morning until late at night, sorting out second-hand clothes for hurricane victims in Central America. Some of these volunteers were over eighty years old, and some were as young as seven. Although it took a lot of time and effort to sort out those clothes, they did their jobs happily and contentedly.

These volunteers also participated in environmental protection work. "You are more than eighty years old," I said to a commissioner. "Are you also an environmental protection volunteer?" "Yes," she replied, "and we have another volunteer who is over ninety years old!"

I then recalled that when I visited them last time, a volunteer who was more than ninety years old came to see me. Although he didn't come this time because he was suffering from a cold, he still sent his greetings to me through a commissioner. "Since he has a cold," I said to them, "you should check on him more often." They nodded their heads and said, "Sure, we often visit him and keep him company."

I was touched when I heard this. Although the volunteer was so advanced in age, he still devoted himself to Tzu Chi and spent a lot of time doing environmental protection work. When he fell ill, our members took care of him as if he were their relative. Full of love and mutual care, their world is so beautiful.

At noon that same day, I went outside to take a look at the neighborhood. Several elderly volunteers walked towards me and said, "So, we finally meet the Master in person."

"Haven't you ever seen me before?" I asked them. "Yes, we see you on Tzu Chi TV every day," they answered, "but we never had the chance to be so close to you and talk to you."

Then they extended their hands to me. "We not only want to talk to you, we would also like to shake hands with you." Their faces were all brimming with contentment and joy. Seeing their bright smiles, I felt warm at heart.

There was one nice old gentleman who said to me, "Oh, I've finally met you, Master!"

"You haven't seen me before?"

"Yes, I have. I've been a Tzu Chi member for more than twenty years!"

"Really?" I said to him. "You've been with us so long? Thank you so much."

"This gentleman is very kind-hearted," a commissioner said. "He's donated a large portion of his earnings to us."

"Grandpa, what do you do for a living?" I asked him.

"I'm the caretaker of a temple and I make NT$15,000 a month [about US$500]."

"Only $15,000? Is that enough to keep you?"

"It's more than I need," he said contentedly. "After deducting my daily expenses from my wages, there's still a lot left over. I donate NT$1,000 [US$33] a month to our foundation for the construction of the hospitals."

"Thank you so much," I said to him. "You really support Tzu Chi."

"It is I who should thank you," he said humbly. "You gave me the chance to do good deeds and to help build the hospitals."

Because he joined Tzu Chi more than twenty years ago, he was one of the earliest donors who had contributed to the construction of the Tzu Chi Hospital in Hualien. Regardless of his old age, he was still energetic and full of spirit. Furthermore, he was still working and had a regular income. Because his life was very simple, he still had extra money to make donations. I was touched to see him give his love so unselfishly.

Many children also came to see me when I was in Ilan. Some were in their mothers' arms, some were led along by their mothers, and some waited in lines along with other adults. Upon seeing me walk in, a little child immediately prostrated himself before me. I noticed that he was very little, so I bent down to ask him, "How old are you?" He raised his head and said, "I'm twee (three)." He spoke with a childish voice and looked very cute.

There was one toddler in his mother's arms. When he saw me, he put his palms together and kept bowing to me. After I walked past them, I turned around to look at them and found that he was still moving his folded hands up and down. I wondered whether these children were reincarnations of Tzu Chi commissioners who had passed away. They all seemed to have come into this world with an inborn faith and love.

Sometimes I would go over to these children and give them a hug. They would lean towards me as if I were very close to them. I had never seen them before—how come they seemed so familiar with me? I could not help asking, "Were you a Tzu Chi commissioner in your previous life? What was your commissioner ID number?"

Looking at these children, I began to envision their future—in ten or twenty years they will grow into young people and dedicate themselves to our society. They have all begun to save money for me and some of them are even Honorary Board members. "Thank you for joining us," I often say to them. "Your timely arrival will contribute to the construction of a better Tzu Chi world."

Look at these Tzu Chi bodhisattvas. They march in a circle—one keeps close to the next in a procession that is never broken. The procession of Tzu Chi will never come to an end, because these children will carry on the work of our elderly volunteers.

Vows Give Strength

People often ask me one question: "What kind of power keeps pushing you forward?" "Love," I always answer. "The Great Love of many people supports me and pushes me forward."

Is there anything in the world more powerful than love? Abiding by Great Love, Tzu Chi people spread their love to every corner of society. When the Vocational Training Bureau of the Council of Labor Affairs held a vocational skills contest for physically challenged people and called for volunteers to help, one hundred Tzu Chi volunteers responded. They took care of the contestants with Great Love and sincere hearts, and the contestants were greatly touched.

One of them, a Mr. Fan, won second place in the contest. He was awarded a silver medal and NT$60,000 [US$2,000]. When he went on stage to deliver his acceptance speech, he said, "I'm really grateful to the government for holding this contest so I could have the chance to win. Since I am able to support myself, I'd like to donate the prize money to Tzu Chi to help those who don't have any means to support themselves."

When he later came to the Abode of Still Thoughts to present the prize money to me, I asked him, "Why do you want to donate the money to Tzu Chi?"

"Tzu Chi has done many things for our society," he replied. "I'm grateful and I'd like to dedicate my little effort to it." He also told me why he entered the contest. "Master, you once said that we do not have the right to own our lives, only the right to use them. I'm physically disabled but my hands are healthy, so I decided to enter the contest. If I won the prize, I would donate the prize money to Tzu Chi."

He made this vow when he made up his mind to enter the contest. Soon afterwards he broke something while he was at work. Taking it as a bad omen, he thought that he might not be able to win the prize and thus felt very depressed. However, the words "Tzu Chi" kept crossing his mind. The thought of Tzu Chi restored his determination. He decided to do his best and concentrate on the contest.

His specialty was fixing watches. But someone told me that he not only fixed watches, he was also a wood sculptor. The components of watches are very small, and it takes a magnifying glass and a lot of patience and care to repair a watch. A lot of work is also required to cut and chisel a piece of wood into a fine piece of sculpture. These two types of work were completely different in nature, but he was good at both. From this we can see that he must have been a hard worker.

Although he was physically challenged, he was mentally healthy and filled with love. Inspired by what I had said—"We do not have the right to own our lives, only the right to use them"—he used his abilities to the utmost and showed Great Love through his actions. After he announced on stage that he would donate his prize money to Tzu Chi, the second runner-up, Miss Chuang, who was good at weaving, also donated her NT$40,000 [US$1,333] award to Tzu Chi. Because she lived in Nantou, in southern Taiwan, I asked a Tzu Chi sister who also lived there to express my gratitude to her.

This is the power of love. In the world of love, there is no discrimination. The love of a person who is physically challenged is as beautiful as that of one who is not. Just like our innate buddha-nature, the power of love never diminishes.

A Contented Couple

Every day, different plays are enacted on the stage of life. Some lives are dull and others full of color, some characters happy and some sad. However they may be, the most important thing in life is to head toward the right direction and not go astray.

One day, a plainly dressed couple came with a commissioner to the Abode of Still Thoughts. They wished to donate an ambulance to the Tzu Chi Hospital. The husband brought NT$800,000 [US$26,666] with him and asked me to accept it. He had originally asked a commissioner to pass it on to me, but the commissioner knew the couple was not very well-off and refused to take the money. The husband then implored another commissioner to bring the money to me.

He used to be a bus driver. To give his family a good life, he worked harder than his colleagues did. Maybe his outstanding performance made some of his colleagues jealous. One day, four or five of them barged onto his bus, beat him up and even slashed him with knives.

It took him a long time to recover. After he was released from the hospital, he went back to work. Feeling that the incident was probably just a bit of bad luck, he did not try to find out the real cause of it and just concentrated on making money for his family. Unfortunately, perhaps due to the heavy psychological and financial pressures he was under, he started to have hallucinations. He was hospitalized again and did not recover until one year later. For the past two years, he had been driving a cab to support his family.

They lived a frugal life. His wife was good and virtuous. No matter what happened to her husband, she always stayed by him and fulfilled her duties faithfully without complaint. After the assault, he realized that an injured person must receive timely medical assistance and that besides supporting his own family he should also do something for society. Thus, he made a commitment to donate an ambulance to our hospital and pushed himself to work even harder. Over a period of time he managed to save NT$800,000.

When I learned about his situation, I told him that I understood his determination to help, but since he was not in good health and his four children were still in school I would be worried if he did not keep part of the money. If he really wanted to make a donation for us to buy an ambulance, he could do so by way of installment payments and one day he would eventually fulfill his wish.

He kept assuring me that there was still money in his savings account and that they only needed to work harder to save more. Finally, he and his wife agreed to take NT$600,000 home.

To them the most important things in life were diligence and good health. This couple was not rich materially, but they were rich spiritually.

Life is like a big stage. Some of us live a prosperous and happy life and some a tough one. No matter how good our life might be, we all have to take the curtain call one day. Although our lives may differ, we are all equally blessed if we are physically and mentally healthy and cheerfully accept what life brings us.

Since we are blessed, we should appreciate what we have and be contented. Although life may bring us pressures, as long as we are open-minded those pressures will dissipate gradually. Take that couple as an example. They went through a lot of difficulties, but they still kept a healthy out-look on life. There are many different roads to take in life and we must choose carefully. Only a simple, serene life will bring us happiness.

The Source of Happiness

Hsieh Kun-shan, a famous Taiwanese artist who paints with his mouth and foot, is an optimistic and industrious person. His arms and one of his legs were amputated after an accident, and the leg that remained had some problems too. However, he is happier and more contented than most people. His spirit touches me greatly.

Twice a month he comes to the Tzu Chi Hospital in Hualien to help patients who have sustained spinal cord injuries or whose limbs have been amputated. Through teaching them to paint by holding brushes with their mouths, he also tries to infuse faith and courage into these patients. In 1997, he went abroad to receive an award given to outstanding handicapped painters. He proved that one's physical condition does not determine what one can achieve.

In the Heart Lotus palliative care ward in the hospital, there is a painting. At first glance it looks like a picture of lotus flowers, but upon closer inspection you will find an indistinct image of the Buddha in it. It was created by Hsieh, and it is the most remarkable work of art I have seen in several decades. Hsieh doesn't have healthy arms and legs and his eyesight is poor. Were it not for his perseverance and hard work, he would never have achieved so much.

I once asked him if he needed his wife to help him with his daily necessities. His wife, who was also present, immediately replied that he didn't need any help and that instead he was the one who helped her. I asked him how he washed himself every morning. He said since he did not have hands and since toothbrushes do not move by themselves, he fastened his toothbrush to a table and moved his head over it. It was amazing how white and shiny his teeth were. Even people who have perfect hands may not be able to keep their teeth so clean and bright.

He mixed powdered milk for his daughter. "Really?" I asked his daughter. "Yes, Daddy always mixes powdered milk for me," the little girl affirmed. Later I suggested that a Tzu Chi TV crew film Mr. Hsieh's daily life. And they did. We saw from the TV program how Hsieh mixed powdered milk for his daughter, folded sheets and mopped floors, just as his wife had told us. It was really some feat.

Who is fortunate? Are people who have lost their limbs unfortunate? There is a Buddhist story about a pair of inseparable twin sisters, the Goddess of Fortune and the Goddess of Disaster. Wherever the Goddess of Fortune goes, the Goddess of Disaster follows. The Buddha once said, "Never pray for any god to help you. What is more important is to bless yourself." Blessings do not come from simply praying to gods. Indeed, that might bring you disasters that often tag along.

Mr. Hsieh's optimism and hard work is a kind of self-blessing. Instead of feeling depressed for what happened to him, he appreciates and cherishes what he still has. He is thus able to lead a harmonious family life and give his love to the needy. His life is full of happiness.

If someone says, "You are very blessed," you should thank them and accept their blessings, instead of retorting, "I don't think so, I'm miserable" [a common Chinese response, perhaps out of fear that the gods might hear and become jealous of one's good fortune]. By doing so, you are pushing away blessings and cursing yourself.

At the Hualien Tzu Chi Hospital, there was an old patient in her seventies who had suffered from diabetes for several decades before it deteriorated into uremia. Our doctor suggested that she have her seriously infected leg amputated, or else the ulceration might put her life at risk. Although the doctor kept trying to persuade her to have her leg amputated, the elderly woman adamantly refused.

She looked distressed all day long. One day a volunteer came to visit, and a patient in the same ward told her, "Please spend some time with her and make her happier. She keeps complaining about how miserable her life is."

The volunteer approached the woman and encouraged her to take a more positive outlook. But the old woman kept crying over her miserable life.

"Why are you miserable?" the volunteer asked her.

"I'm already over seventy and I still need to have my leg amputated."

"But grandma, your legs have served you for more than seventy years," the volunteer observed. "They've done their jobs. You should be grateful for your legs and consider yourself rather fortunate."

After pondering, the woman smiled through her tears. "You're right, I've used my legs for more than seventy years. I should be grateful for that. Thanks! I am indeed lucky!"

Two days later, another woman who was seriously ill came to stay in the same ward. She kept crying even after our doctor had treated her. A volunteer asked her what the problem was. The woman said all her sons were dead and she only had six daughters left, and she lamented over the unfairness of life.

The first old woman heard this and immediately said to this woman, "Don't feel that way. We should say our life is good to bless ourselves." The woman who had been complaining was now able to help others because she looked at life from a different angle.

Indeed, how we feel depends on how we look at things. We should believe in blessing ourselves. Grumbling will only make our lives more miserable. But if we bless ourselves and look on the bright side, we will live happily. Let's wish each other well and appreciate, cherish and cultivate our blessings.

Saving a Life Feels Great

Although modern science is so advanced, the only cure for leukemia is still a bone marrow transplant.

Marrow donation started several decades ago in Western countries. People in the West are more open-minded about organ donations, so when their nations promote marrow donation they are often active supporters. However, reports show that some volunteers still back out when notified that they have been identified as suitable donors. People in Taiwan are more conservative toward donating their bodies or organs. Some of them instinctively reject the idea of marrow donation, because they believe it will put their lives at risk.

However an event prompted Tzu Chi to set up the Tzu Chi Taiwan Marrow Donor Registry. One day, our US branch office received a request to find a compatible marrow donor for an overseas Chinese female in the States. The woman had obtained her master's degree and planned to pursue her doctorate. Unfortunately, she was diagnosed with leukemia and was in dire need of a bone marrow transplant.

Because bone marrow matching involves factors such as genes and racial background, it was simply out of the question for her to receive a transplant of bone marrow donated by a Caucasian. She thus asked our US Free Clinic for help. We solicited bone marrow donor registrations and also put on a concert, the proceeds of which would be used to assist her. After this experience, I felt that modern medical technology like bone marrow transplants should also be made available to people in Taiwan to improve the quality of local medical treatment and to help victims of blood diseases on the island.

When the Buddha was still alive, he once said, "I am willing to give my head, eyes, marrow or brain to other people." When I read this passage a long time ago, I doubted whether it was possible for the organs of one person to be transplanted into the body of another. I never thought that after I became a nun, I would begin to do charity work and build hospitals and would therefore come in touch with advanced medical information which helped me better understand the Buddha's teachings.

The year after our Hualien Tzu Chi Hospital opened, we set up a "bone bank" in which donated bones could be stored for fifteen years for future use. Some time later, I called for the establishment of a bone marrow donor data bank. To my delight, many people responded to my call.

I asked people who had signed up what they were donating. They were not certain, but they believed that I would not harm a healthy person in order to save the life of a sick person.

More than eight hundred people signed up within just three days of my first appeal. Since then, we have continued launching marrow donor registration campaigns. By the end of April 2001, the data bank listed about 210,000 people—the largest data bank in Asia. In addition, once suitable donors are found, they rarely back out. But as for other countries, I have heard that there are still a large number of listed volunteer donors who renege on donating their marrow.

I still remember that on November 11, 1997, a young man came to the Tzu Chi Hospital to donate his marrow for a recipient in Guangzhou, China. Later, he came to the Abode of Still Thoughts in the company of a commissioner.

I praised and thanked the donor for being such a bodhisattva, for although he did not leave Taiwan he saved a life in
Guangzhou. However, the young man expressed his gratitude to me for setting up our Tzu Chi Marrow Donor Registry, which made it possible for him to save someone. He
exclaimed, "It feels so good to save someone's life!" His
response deeply touched me.

The marrow recipient was an eleven-year-old boy in
Guangzhou. He was a top student, well liked by his teachers
and classmates. But unfortunately he was afflicted with
leukemia, and to make matters even worse his family was
quite poor.

The boy's doctor told his parents that a bone marrow
transplant was imperative to save the boy. The monthly
income of the family was 800 Renminbi [US$95], which was
far from enough to cover the family's daily expenses, let alone
the medical bills incurred by the boy. Therefore, the boy's
school organized a fund-raising drive and raised 10,000 Renminbi [US$1,230] for him. But it was still not enough. At the
end of his rope, his father told the hospital that he would sell
his organs to raise money for his son.

After waiting a long time to find a compatible donor, a
schoolteacher was found, but the teacher was unwilling to
donate his marrow. "I had my blood tested to see if I could
save my brother, but my brother died before he could undergo the transplant operation. Why should I donate my marrow now?"

A doctor in Guangzhou who had visited Tzu Chi before
contacted us for help. Luckily, a match was found in just a
few days. Upon hearing that he could save a life, the donor

immediately came to our hospital to have his marrow extracted. His altruistic spirit was truly admirable.

It is really too bad that society today lacks trust. Such an ill social climate is truly worrisome. When the Buddha came to the world in human form, his mission was to cleanse our minds and activate our love, so that there would be mutual trust, help and love between people and we could all live happily. How to live at ease and in joy? As long as we can give without demanding anything in return, we will be able to live with peace of mind.

Delivering Marrow across the Taiwan Straits

If we hope that the world can be filled with light, we must set people's love in motion. When the love of each individual is united together, there will be Great Love, which will light up our world.

The wife of Dr. Li Cheng-tao [head of the Tzu Chi Marrow Donation Registry] once shared with us her experience of delivering marrow to China. She said as soon as she got off the plane, a swarm of reporters surrounded her. The superintendent of the hospital to which she was delivering the marrow and the recipient's family also came to greet her at the airport.

The recipient, a prosecuting attorney, was less than thirty years old. He was also a victim of leukemia and needed a marrow transplant to survive. His only hope was a compatible donor living in Taiwan. The donor was like a compassionate bodhisattva. He not only came willingly to our hospital to have his marrow extracted, but he also sincerely prayed that the recipient would recover after the transplant. What pure, selfless Great Love the donor demonstrated!

There was a patient in Germany who asked a donor listed in our Marrow Donor Registry to give marrow for the second time. The donor agreed without the least bit of hesitation. The day after his marrow was extracted, the donor, accompanied by our marrow donor care team, came to the Abode of Still Thoughts to visit me. The moment I saw him I knew he must be the one, so I asked him directly if he was the donor. He replied that he was. I praised him as a truly kind man and asked him if he knew who the recipient was. He shook his head. "It's not important who I donate my marrow to; what is important is that my marrow can save that person." Then I asked him if he felt unwell after the marrow extraction. He replied that it was the second time he had donated marrow, and he did not feel any discomfort.

I did not know that it was the second time he donated his marrow, which was very rare indeed. A member of the marrow donor care team explained that the recipient recovered very well two years ago after the first transplant operation, but recently he had a cold and was plagued by a persistent fever. When the hospital staff examined him again, they found that two important elements were missing in his blood. That's why they asked the donor to donate his marrow again.

I was touched when I heard the story, so I told the donor that I was grateful to him and that he was truly a living bodhisattva, for although he was in Taiwan he saved a Chinese man in Germany. The young man replied that he was the one who should be grateful to Tzu Chi for setting up the marrow donor registry and giving him the chance to save a person's life. "Master, it is I who should feel grateful to you," he said. Though founded in Taiwan, Tzu Chi spreads love all over the world and we are therefore able to witness the deeds of many living bodhisattvas.

This donor did not know whose life he was going to save, but he was willing to give again and again. The selfless Great Love he demonstrated was the incarnation of the Three Conditions of Emptiness in Buddhism—no giver, no receiver, no material to be given away. [Once donors have given to charity, they no longer think about the donation so they won't brag about it or cling to it. They see no recipients or things to be given away.] This young man's reply—"It's not important who I donate my marrow to; what is important is that my marrow can save that person"—showed us that he didn't think of himself as a savior, and more importantly he didn't dwell on the marrow he gave to the patient.

It's not easy for people to agree to have their marrow extracted. If a person doesn't have a healthy mindset or sufficient wisdom or knowledge, it will be difficult to accept the very concept of marrow donation, let alone agree to donate his or her own marrow. Therefore, what that donor did— donating his marrow twice—was really rare. His actions exemplified the Three Conditions of Emptiness, which is something we should keep in mind while walking on the Path of the Bodhisattvas.

Here is another example. A patient who lived in the United States needed marrow. A married woman who had emigrated from Taiwan to the States donated her marrow to him. She was very young and had a five-year-old son.

When her son was born, he was diagnosed with an abnormal heart valve. The boy was therefore unable to engage in daily activities. In the past five years, he had seven operations. When this young mother learned that she was a compatible donor, she was very happy. In order to maintain her health to ensure a successful transplant, she started taking nutritional supplements. However, it turned out that she was allergic to the supplements and her whole body swelled up.

The patient's family and doctor became nervous, fearing that she might change her mind because of her unfavorable condition. Dr. Li Cheng-tao's wife, who was at our US marrow data bank center at that time, contacted the young mother to inquire whether she was still willing to donate her marrow. She told us that she wanted the transplant to succeed so much that she had taken the nutritional supplements to make herself healthier, and her allergic reaction would not stop her from donating her marrow. As the mother of a son who was often ill, she understood the agonies of a mother seeing her ailing child in pain. So she was still firm about donating her marrow.

What was amazing was that a few days after she made up her mind to donate her marrow, she was informed that her son, who was receiving special care in an intensive care unit, was well enough to leave the hospital. The boy has made a speedy recovery ever since. He is now attending kindergarten and is a healthy, vigorous, lovely boy.

This mother's husband told us, "If my wife is found to be a suitable donor again, I will encourage her to donate her marrow again." Indeed, we can save lives through marrow donation without hurting our health at all, so why don't we do it?

Springtime for the Elderly

I have always hoped that our volunteers will undertake community volunteer work and take care of lonely, elderly people. Thus I asked Tzu Chi commissioners to collect data on senior citizens who lived alone in their areas. Within a short time, all the relevant information was gathered and compiled. Then I asked the commissioners to implement the community care system, pay visits to every household to see if the old people needed help, and encourage healthy old people to help others in need.

Our commissioners were quick to act, and soon I began to receive their reports. Through their visits, they found many old folks in need of help. Some were bedridden, incontinent and unable to prepare meals for themselves. The houses of these people were very dirty because no one cleaned them. Upon learning of the condition of these old people, our Tzu Chi commissioners and Tzu Cheng Faith Corps members pitched in to help. They cleaned their houses and yards, bathed them, and cut their hair and nails.

Touched by the dedication of these volunteers, a neighbor of an old man who lived alone said, "I know that Tzu Chi commissioners are all very busy and have a lot of duties on their hands, but they still come regularly to care for my neighbor. I think I should share some of their burden."

This kind-hearted neighbor volunteered to take care of the old man. Because he was also a Tzu Chi member, our commissioners entrusted the old man to him. A few days later, the neighbor phoned one of our commissioners and said that the old man was running a fever. The commissioner immediately offered to take him to the hospital. To her surprise, this member told the commissioner not to worry for he just wanted to let her know about the condition, and he said he would take the man to the hospital himself.

I felt warm and touched to know that the Tzu Chi commissioners' regular visits to lonely senior citizens had inspired many other people to care for their elderly neighbors.

There was an old soldier who was close to eighty years old and who lived alone in a veterans' community. He was sick, malodorous, and stayed in a dirty and unkempt house. When our commissioners learned about his situation, they went to see if he needed any help. The old man's neighbor, an old veteran in his seventies who was still healthy and hearty, also volunteered to help him. The neighbor said he was ashamed of himself, for although they were neighbors and both of them were veterans he seldom dropped in on him to see how he was doing. He said that from then on, he would visit the sick man more often to keep him company, give him a hand and cook for him.

Tzu Chi volunteers set an example for healthy elderly people to care for other old people who are in poor health. When people can care for and help each other, a closely-knit and self-supporting community will come into being.

The implementation of a community care system is necessary. Through their service, Tzu Chi members bridge the distance between the inhabitants of a community. When we care lovingly for the elderly and help them in whatever way we can, their neighbors will see it and realize that neighbors are far more important than distant relatives in times of need. When neighbors reach out to help each other, they will get along with each other better. If all of us can show respect and care to senior citizens as if they were our own relatives, there will be no neglected, lonely old people in our society.

Humanitarian Care Transcends All Borders

When we love others, we are also cultivating blessings for ourselves. Many people in Taiwan are willing to give their love to others, making the island a fortunate place.

In October 1998, heavy rains brought on by two consecutive typhoons caused serious flooding in northern Taiwan. Fortunately, the floods receded in a short time and many people went to the disaster areas to help the victims. For example, over one thousand Tzu Chi volunteers helped city workers and military forces clean up debris in Hsichih. They finished the herculean job in just one day. At roughly the same time, another typhoon attacked the Philippines, and hurricanes ravaged Honduras and the Dominican Republic.

The Dominican Republic, a place where the distribution of wealth is severely unequal, has rich people but far more poor ones. After the hurricane, Tzu Chi members in the United States visited the disaster areas to inspect the damage and distribute relief goods. Local Chinese people from China and Taiwan all volunteered to assist us.

Some of them said that they had heard of Tzu Chi when they were still living in Taiwan, but they never had the chance to participate in Tzu Chi activities. After they emigrated to Central America, they had little chance of joining Tzu Chi. Others said that although they had never heard of the foundation when they were in Taiwan, they heard a lot about our international relief work from the media after they went abroad.

They all said that they had long wanted to join Tzu Chi, but never expected that they would finally get in touch with us when we were doing relief work in the Dominican Republic. They joined us in our relief efforts and had a great time helping other people.

When I called for an island-wide clothing drive for Central American hurricane victims, many people in Taiwan donated their used clothes. Some of the clothes were brand-new. Thanks to their generosity, many Central American hurricane victims survived the winter. What a charitable act!

Some commissioners later told me that the cargo containers we had reserved were not enough for the clothes we had collected and a lot more clothes were still pouring in. I told them that since these clothes bore evidence of people's love, we should take them all in even if we would have to reserve more containers to deliver them to the victims.

Besides the victims in the Dominican Republic, the Honduran victims needed clothes as well. In Honduras, people were already poor before the hurricanes struck. Some local women didn't even have blankets to wrap their newborn babies in, and they had to use old newspapers instead. It is hard for us who have grown up in a good environment to imagine what it was like.

Tzu Chi started its international relief work mainly to encourage all Tzu Chi members around the globe to dedicate their efforts to local charity work and to fulfill their duty as global citizens. Take the Tzu Chi US chapter as an example. They not only care for the elderly and sick in their communities, but also help other countries plagued by disasters. Although these Tzu Chi members live abroad, their love for Taiwan has never faded. They try their best to improve Taiwan's international image through their charitable efforts, hoping that their native country can win recognition from the international community. Thus every time they engage in a relief operation, they never forget to raise a red banner inscribed with "Tzu Chi Foundation, Taiwan" at their distribution site.

We still have a long way to go in enveloping the world with Great Love. We need to work closely together and give unceasingly to implement our four missions of charity, medical care, educational development, and cultural promotion.

The goal of medical work is to save lives. Nothing in the world is more precious than life. So Tzu Chi has built hospitals, and in the future two more Tzu Chi hospitals will be constructed in Hsintien, northern Taiwan, and Tantzu, central Taiwan. It takes all our love and efforts to make the construction of these hospitals possible.

We must not slow our steps in carrying out our educational and cultural missions either. For the benefit of the next generation, let's all work diligently to improve the quality of our education and to establish a culture of love. Let us bring love to every corner of the world and help all those in need.

Self-Enhancement

The Buddha's teaching is like nectar which steadily soothes the burning of our hearts. When dealing with matters in life, the more ordinary they are, the more effort we should put into learning how to handle them smoothly. The better we learn, the lighter our hearts will become.

The Prince Who Steadfastly Guarded His Mind

The most important things in our life's journey are to have the right views and to be single-minded in attaining our objectives. In this way, we will not go astray in the pursuit of our ideals. As the saying goes, "There is but one step from the sublime to the ridiculous." This shows that guarding our minds is crucial.

Consider the case of Sakyamuni Buddha. Before he left home to become a monk, he was Prince Siddhartha, who enjoyed all sorts of worldly pleasures in his palace. He was dearly loved by his father, King Suddhodana, and his aunt, who was also his foster mother, and he was respected by all the people in his kingdom. To many people this would seem to be a wonderful life, but Prince Siddhartha did not want such things. He was aware of the impermanence and changes in life, as reflected in aging, illness and death. He was able to contemplate and pursue the truth of the world. This is the difference between an enlightened person and ordinary people.

Most people are easily influenced by the things around them. They immerse themselves in their own sensual pleasures, oblivious to the grief and pain of others. Their worlds are centered on themselves, not others. That's what makes them ordinary. But Prince Siddhartha was different. Although he enjoyed a royal lifestyle, he was fully aware of the problems faced by other people. Besides the suffering of aging, illness and death, Indians of that time endured the caste system, which he regarded as unfair. There was also poverty and other human tragedies, as well as natural disasters such as floods, hurricanes and droughts. The problems caused by environmental and social changes were always on his mind. What was the solution to these problems?

One day, the prince finally asked his father for permission to leave home to undertake his spiritual cultivation. This was a devastating blow for the king. Indeed, as Asita the sage had predicted when Siddhartha was born, the prince would either be a great ruler of the world, or he would be an Enlightened Teacher for all the people and all the celestial beings of the universe if he chose to become a monk.

The king had mixed feelings when he first heard this prediction. He was happy that the prince might one day succeed to his throne and rule the kingdom. He was concerned that his son would renounce his lay life and become a monk, even though he was aware that attaining enlightenment was not a bad thing to do. Although these thoughts had been with him all these years, the king was nevertheless shocked when Siddhartha finally expressed his wish to leave home. The king told his son, "The kingdom and the people will need your leadership. How can you abandon them? Furthermore, a king's position is a highly respectable one. When you rule the kingdom in the future, you can freely fulfill your aspiration to save the world."

"A life full of material, tangible things is hard to change," the prince replied. "The suffering of birth, aging, sickness and death cannot be resolved simply by changing the environment."

"Can you bear to leave your parents? To leave your wife Yasodhara and your son Rahula?"

"Worldly love is hard to abandon. But Father, if you can resolve these issues that are bothering me, I will not leave home."

Thereupon, the king asked, "What can you not resolve?"

"Father, if you can let me not grow old, not be ill, not die, and not experience the agony of parting with people I love, I will put aside my plans to practice spiritual cultivation."

"There are no solutions for these," the king replied despondently. "Man will naturally grow old with time. Who does not grow old? The body does not necessarily need to grow old to be inflicted with illnesses. Rich or poor, everyone will get ill. I am no exception. One day, I too will die…"

"Yes, not only will you go through these sufferings, but so will everyone else," the prince said. "Just as you cannot bear to see me leave, the parting of two lovers is also painful. But eternal parting due to death is even more painful. There are so many forms of suffering in our lives. How do we resolve them?"

When the king heard this, he knew he could not answer his son's questions. "Father, you love me so much but you still cannot solve my problems," the prince pleaded. "All the sufferings that I just mentioned are so unbearable. Hence, I must engage in profound soul-searching to seek the Truth that leads to the cessation of these sufferings."

No one could dissuade the prince from his intentions, and he finally left home. If Prince Siddhartha had not been firm in his convictions and bravely overcome all obstacles, how would we have our Fundamental Teacher, Sakyamuni Buddha?

After overcoming many trials and tribulations, Prince Siddhartha attained enlightenment and taught the world what he had learned in as clear a manner as possible. For example, he taught people that to ensure their rebirth as humans in their next life, they should observe the Five Precepts of no killing, stealing, fornicating, lying, or drinking alcohol. He taught people to practice the Ten Acts of Goodness[1] in order to be reincarnated in heaven; to practice the Eight Noble Paths[2] to remove ignorance and bad habits; and to practice the Six Paramitas[3] in order to transcend life and death and finally become a saint.

We need Right Thought and Right View to guide our lives. The Buddha's wisdom can lead us towards goodness and attain bliss. We need to have proper control of our thoughts so that we can head unfalteringly towards our goal.

---

[1] The Ten Acts of Goodness refer to abstention from killing, stealing, fornicating, lies, double-talking, abusive speech, flattery, greed, anger and delusion.

[2] The Eight Noble Paths refer to eight ways practiced by the spiritually cultivated to attain liberation. They consist of Right View, Right Thought, Right Speech, Right Behavior, Right Livelihood, Right Effort, Right Mindfulness, and Right Contemplation.

[3] The Six Paramitas are ways of practicing the dharma: charity, keeping the precepts, tolerating insults, diligence, contemplation, and wisdom. These allow the practitioner to cross from the shore of suffering and reincarnation to the other shore of nirvana and joy.

Unleashing Our Compassion

There is a Chinese saying: "It is often too late for children to show filial piety towards their parents." It is very unfortunate when our parents cannot live long enough for us to show them our respect and love. In the sutras, we see how Maudgalyayana went to hell to save his mother and how Sakyamuni Buddha went to heaven to expound his teachings to his mother. Even if one has attained buddhahood, one should practice filial piety promptly to avoid having regrets later.

Before the Buddha entered nirvana, he felt that there was still one thing he needed to take care of. Hence, he used his supernatural powers to ascend to the Trayastrimsa Heaven where he lectured on his teachings to his mother.

What is supernatural power? Many people may think that this refers to the power of levitation or the power to pass through solid objects. Actually, supernatural power is the wisdom inherent in all people. When we are connected with this intrinsic wisdom, we will naturally acquire supernatural powers. But even supernatural powers cannot overcome the power of karma. Hence, even if we acquire supernatural powers, we cannot abuse them and create bad karma.

The *Precious Ornament Sutra* says, "Our intrinsic wisdom can help us eradicate all obstructions." When our intrinsic wisdom is activated, there will be no impediments whether we are in heaven or hell. The purpose of learning the dharma is to realize this wisdom. It is not easy for most people, but it is attainable if we concentrate our minds.

According to Buddhist scriptures, there are six kinds of supernatural powers: supernatural mobility—the ability to freely come and go, despite physical barriers such as mountains, rivers, and the earth; supernatural sight—the ability to see beyond that which can be perceived by the human eye; supernatural hearing—the ability to hear clearly and without distortion and to understand the languages of all living beings; supernatural clairvoyance—the ability to know the past, present and future; and supernatural telepathy—the ability to clearly read other's minds. These abilities are not rare, since they are attainable by practitioners of other religions and even by ghosts and deities. Most people must speak out their thoughts to let other people know what they are thinking about. However, what they say is only a fraction of what is really on their minds.

Those who want to learn Buddhism may also learn the sixth supernatural power, absence of afflictions. By only using their naked eyes, many people do not see the true nature of things. They are misled by external appearances and thus develop afflictions. This is because their eyes are defiled. Their ears are also defiled and they are easily distracted by sounds, not realizing that what they hear is gossip and falsehood. They slacken and their resolution to practice spiritual cultivation deteriorates. All this gives rise to ignorance, attachments and confusion in their minds. Absence of afflictions is the realization of our true nature. It is attained when we are free of greed, anger, delusion, arrogance and doubt. It is the true purpose of our spiritual cultivation. If the mind has afflictions, any supernatural powers acquired will also be tainted and defiled. If the mind is pure, it is not difficult to know the past or present. The problem, though, is that most people are swayed by what they see and hear. If people are misled by what appears before them at the present moment, how can they accurately perceive the past or the future?

The Buddha cultivated himself to the stage where he was totally unattached to anything in this world. He could employ his inherent boundless wisdom to ascend to heaven, descend to hell, or roam the earth. We should build a strong foundation when learning Buddhism and learn to cultivate compassion and wisdom in our daily lives. Compassion is Great Love— when we love all living beings in the world, we will naturally have hearts completely filled with great filial piety.

Recently, many college students volunteering in our hospitals shared with us their experiences in observing the impermanence and suffering associated with birth, aging, illness and death. They deeply felt the urgency of doing good deeds and observing filial piety. One of their observations was that in learning to serve others, we should begin by serving our parents. We must not wait till our parents are ill, old or dead before we remember to show our respect for them. If these students can appreciate this point, they can take immediate steps to practice filial piety.

The Buddha's mind is basically a filial mind. The *Sutra of Profound Gratitude to Parents* says that when the Buddha saw a pile of white bones on the side of the road, he immediately knew that they belonged to his parents from his previous lives. Motivated by his filial piety, the Buddha returned to the world to teach the dharma to mankind. This shows that filial piety is the root of humanity. If we disregard filial piety, there will be no other virtuous practices to follow. A mind of great filial piety is a mind of Great Love, a virtue we should always practice.

Time and Tide Wait for No One

We are only young once in this lifetime. If we want to be young again, we will have to wait till our next rebirth. Hence, we should treasure our lives. Whether we are young, middle-aged or old, we should make the best use of our abilities because we cannot turn back the wheel of time and become young again. Birth, aging, illness and death are natural processes in life that all living beings, even the Buddha and his disciples, must go through.

When the Buddha was growing old, there were several things that concerned him, including the issue of being separated from friends and loved ones by death. At that time, his old disciple Sariputra died from an illness in Rajagrha. A young monk named Cunda brought Sariputra's belongings—his clothes and alms bowl—to Jetavana. There, Cunda saw Ananda and told him the news of Sariputra's death. Ananda sadly said, "This is grave news, and we should give Sariputra's possessions to the Buddha." With heavy hearts, Ananda and Cunda went before the Buddha and proceeded to explain the situation.

Ananda said to the Buddha, "When I heard about it, I was very sad," and he broke into tears. Ananda was a sentimental person and had been very good friends with Sariputra, who had devotedly shouldered the responsibility of spreading the Buddha's teachings.

"Birth, aging, illness and death are natural occurrences," the Buddha told Ananda. "Why are you so sad?"

"Oh, Buddha," Ananda replied, "your mission to save all living beings is so burdensome. If Sariputra were alive, he could continue to help you. But he's gone now, and you have one fewer disciple to share the load. Of course, I am very sad."

"Ananda, when a tree starts to wilt, it does not necessarily begin from its roots," the Buddha responded. "Sometimes, it starts from its leaves, which turn yellow and drop off. It is true that I am still alive on this earth, and that I need people to help spread my teachings. However, a man's lifespan depends on his karmic conditions in this world. Sariputra's death is like a tree branch that is beginning to wilt. The stages of human life, and indeed the truth pertaining to all living beings, are the same. Who do we count on? No one else but ourselves! All of you have to think of yourselves and my teachings as rafts. The world is like a vast ocean, and it is difficult to navigate from this shore of suffering to the far shore of liberation. But everyone has to do his best and work together to propel the raft forward. In sum, put your mind and efforts to everything you do."

"The buddha-nature is inherent in everyone," the Buddha continued. "Therefore, take refuge in the buddha within you, the dharma within you, the sangha within you. You should attain realization on your own and not rely on others." This is the essence of the Buddha's teachings, and everyone should make the best use of the present moment to practice them.

The spring season goes and returns, but not a person's youth. There is no second spring in our life's journey. Hence, treasure every moment. The Buddha and his disciples were no different—they also had to go through the life cycle of youth, middle age, old age, and eventual nirvana. But they knew how to make the most of every moment, pursue the truth of the universe while young, work at spreading that truth in their middle age, and continue to practice the truth diligently in their old age. We should also make good use of our time, use our abilities for virtuous purposes, and develop life to its fullest extent.

Suffering and Happiness Are in the Mind

What is suffering? What is happiness? There is no benchmark against which to measure these attributes. The feeling of happiness or joy varies from person to person. Some people say, "Life is indeed happy—how could it be suffering?" Yet, others feel that life is indeed suffering. Whether one perceives happiness or suffering is based on one's mind-set.

During the Buddha's time, there were over a thousand monks in his congregation. With this large number of disciples, it was natural that they had all different faculties for learning the Buddha's teachings. Some immediately understood what the Buddha said. They remained calm and were not influenced by either suffering or happiness. Thus, they were able to resolutely practice the dharma. However, there were also sangha members with lower aptitudes who continued to be tortured with unnecessary worries and afflictions despite the Buddha's earnest advice and guidance.

One day, the Buddha passed by a group of monks and heard them talking about how they first decided to shave their heads and become monks because of the afflictions they endured. "When I was a layman, I could not control my sexual desire whenever I saw a woman," one monk said. "Hence, I felt that lust and abstinence both upset me. I shaved my head because I intended to purify my mind. However, even though I have vowed to live up to the precepts, my salacious mind is still difficult to control."

"As a layman I went through many difficulties, and I was unable to feed and clothe myself," another monk said. "I worried about whether I could harvest my crops when there was a drought, or whether my rice fields would be flooded when there was too much rain. Hence, I felt that the greatest suffering was starvation. Now that I am a monk, I no longer need to worry about lack of food."

"I have an incorrigible bad temper," yet another monk added, "and I often fly off the handle. If the attitudes or words of others displease me, I throw a tantrum and start to yell at them, or I even go so far as to beat them up. The Buddha's teachings are good, and I made up my mind to stay in his congregation and accept his teachings in an attempt to break my bad habit. However, bad habits are hard to change. Even though I try my best to control my bad temper, I still give those who displease me a good tongue-lashing. Trying to restrain my temper causes me much suffering."

Another monk stated, "I am most bothered by the cycle of birth, aging, illness and death. We become ugly when we grow old and suffer pain when we fall ill. What causes me the most anxiety is that we don't know when we will die. The Buddha taught us that the world is impermanent and that the land is fragile. I am very worried about when the world will fall into chaos, and I live in fear every day. The Buddha is almighty and within the sangha my mind can be at ease, so I decided to renounce the world and become a monk. However, I still have afflictions, not knowing when I will get sick and die."

At this point of the discussion, the Buddha walked towards them and said, "It is very good that all of you know what suffering is. However, you only know the feeling of suffering, but not its roots. To completely eliminate suffering, you need to trace its cause."

When the monks heard this, they asked the Buddha to explain the origin of suffering. The Buddha said, "The major shortcoming of human life is that humans have bodies and minds that react easily to the external environment. For example, a man has thoughts of lust when he sees an attractive woman. People feel hungry because of the need to feed the physical body. Similarly, people get angry because they fail to discipline their emotions and cannot accommodate others. Thus, suffering comes from the body and mind. The sensation of happiness arises in a similar way."

The Buddha went on. "Why is there fear? It is because of excessive love of one's physical body. Birth, aging, illness and death are natural phenomena, just as there are four seasons in nature. The deluded are attached to their bodies, and as a result their minds become fearful and restless. Suffering comes from the body and mind. If we can treat our bodies as mere vehicles that we should use for doing our spiritual cultivation, we can transform suffering into happiness and convert conditions leading to suffering into ones leading to joy."

The suffering we experience comes from the senses of the body and mind which, however, change all the time. If our minds can be pure and have fewer desires, we can be immune from the suffering arising from sexual desire. We will not be tortured with suffering if we are satisfied with a simple life and do not get angry because of abusive words and unfriendly facial expressions of other people. Hence, I always remind all of us to be mindful of our thoughts and words.

Flowers Bloom and Wilt

Many people are familiar with the concept of the impermanence of life, but few can truly appreciate its profound meaning. Even fewer can keep its meaning in mind. However, impermanence is one of the most important things that a Buddhist has to learn.

One day, when the Buddha was at Jetavana, his disciple Radha came to him. "Buddha, I often hear you expound the principle of impermanence to us. Although I hear it every day, I still do not understand the relation between this principle and our spiritual cultivation."

"Impermanence is the foundation of the philosophy I teach," the Buddha replied. "There is no way you can progress in your understanding of the essence of my teaching if you do not know what impermanence implies. So listen carefully. The Five Aggregates—form, sensation, perception, impulse and consciousness—are impermanent. Do you understand?"

Radha scratched his head. "Buddha, form refers to all that we can see. But the many things I see every day remain the same. Why is form impermanent?"

"Have you seen a flower bud before it blooms? Have you seen the flower after it blooms?"

Radha replied, "Yes, but the bud, the blooming flower, the wilting flower—aren't they all flowers?"

"Yes, they are called 'flowers,' but their names and appearances are different."

"Buddha, I still cannot figure out what this really means," Radha admitted.

"That is because you have not given it good thought," the Buddha said. "You need to feel and experience more deeply. When you see a flower bloom, contemplate on why the flower is blooming. When you see buds, think about why the flower is budding. In fact, try to investigate the flower's original form before its seed germinates and its buds appear."

Radha again scratched his head. "Are you referring to the seed?"

"Yes. Before the flower takes its shape, it starts off as a seed. When the seed is planted in the soil and the conditions are right, it will germinate, grow a stem, develop buds, and bloom. It will then wilt, and seeds will form and fall to the soil. This is the cycle of impermanence."

"Buddha, this is too profound," Radha protested. "How should I perceive this?"

"Do so mindfully," the Buddha said. "Contemplate and understand. Everything in this world is impermanent, and everything changes in cycles. Everything is like seeds which germinate, grow, bloom and wilt as a result of being exposed to the conditions of the sun, soil and air. Through their actions, words and thoughts, people create the seeds of their karma. In the end, they go back into the cycle of rebirth with these seeds of karma. Understanding that a seed planted into the soil will continuously change is only the first step. Continue to be mindful and observe everything that happens around you, and you will understand the meaning of life."

If you can understand impermanence and apply it towards everything in your daily life, there will be nothing to get upset about. If you can be more open-minded and use your body to its full potential, you will gain even further insights.

Human life is like passing the test of time—every second and every minute that goes by accumulates to become time. The fortunes and karma in life also accumulate with time. When you are truly at peace with people, events, and the world, it is a reflection that you have fully understood the impermanence of life. Then you can be released from physical and spiritual suffering and feel at ease at all times.

A Scholar's Dream

Humans pass through four phases in life: childhood, youth, middle age, and old age. Each year the four seasons come and go in the same cycle. However, human life lasts only a few decades. How many seasons will one see?

From the perspective of the Buddha, human life is too short. Even if we live a hundred years, what contributions can we make in this time? Can we fully appreciate the meaning of life? It seems very hard to do.

There is a verse from a Buddhist sutra: "You dream in the time it takes to cook sorghum; you awaken and the sorghum has not yet been eaten." This refers to the following story.

A scholar wanted to go to the capital to participate in the imperial civil service examination held personally by the emperor. He had to travel for several months, a long and arduous journey. One day, he arrived at a small town not too far from the capital, and he decided to rest for a while. He went into a small restaurant and ordered a bowl of sorghum and some other dishes.

While the waiter hurried off to prepare the meal, the scholar thought, "Soon I will be taking the imperial examination. Will I ace the exam and become the highest ranking scholar in the whole nation?"

Because the journey had been long and tiring, the scholar rested his head on the table and before long fell asleep. In his dreams, he saw himself arriving at the capital, entering the examination hall, and winning the highest accolades! He then went to thank the leading examination officer, who, thinking that the scholar was a fine young man, subsequently gave him his daughter's hand in marriage. The scholar married and had sons. Gradually, his sons grew to be handsome men and he himself became old. On his eightieth birthday, his sons, daughters-in-law and grandchildren all came to offer him their congratulations. While he was basking in the bliss of his family, he suddenly heard someone calling and he woke up with a start. It was the waiter with the bowl of sorghum, urging him to wake up and eat the food while it was still hot and fresh. As the scholar woke up from his dream and saw the bowl of sorghum, he realized that it had all been only a dream and he had not even eaten.

At this moment, he suddenly had a revelation: "These dreams of a wonderful life all happened in the time it took to cook a bowl of sorghum. Life is as short as a dream. Do I want to pursue all this? If my life is like the dream I just had, what meaning will it have? Seasons come and go, and life is too short to fuss about anything." At that moment, he attained a profound understanding of the meaning of life.

Although the scholar's dream was short, it was a very pleasant one with no hardships. However, to what extent can life be that smooth in reality? Life is full of obstacles and challenges and innumerable afflictions. Because human life is full of difficulties, some people say, "Human life is filled with suffering and little joy—it is not easy to live through."

We need to understand the true meaning of life. How long we live is unimportant. What is most important is that in our journey through this world, we realize the true value of life and do as many good deeds as we can. There is no meaning if we just lead a muddled life. Even if we live to a hundred years old or longer, life will be meaningless if it is as empty and illusory as a dream.

The four seasons come and go. Human life also passes through the four stages of childhood, youth, middle age and old age. But once past, it is impossible to return to the previous stages. Hence, we should treasure every stage of our lives, understand the meaning of life, and make the most of our abilities to help others. Our physical bodies will come and go, but our wisdom will last forever.

We must make proper use of life, since it lasts only a few decades and is as short as a dream. Thus, it is important to wake up quickly and not continue daydreaming. Only then will we be able to enjoy the springtime of our wisdom life.

Looking for a Witness

In our daily encounters with others, we frequently discriminate or make distinctions between them but fail to examine ourselves.

The Buddha often urged his disciples to meditate on the vileness of all things. This was relatively easy to do in India because Indians customarily practiced "sky burials," whereby human carcasses were taken to the wilderness and left to decompose and to serve as food for birds and other scavengers.

Once, there was a monk who frequently walked back and forth on farm fields. The farmer was very curious about this. He wondered why the man did not spend time on his spiritual cultivation but chose instead to wander through his fields. One day, he saw the monk walking in his fields again. He stopped him and asked, "Why do you come here every day?"

The monk said, "Because I'm looking for some witnesses to testify on my behalf." The farmer did not understand and asked him to explain. The monk replied, "Please come with me and see these honest witnesses."

The farmer followed the monk, and they came to a wild place littered with white bones and foul-smelling human bodies. Birds fed on the carcasses while the monk stood, attentively watching them.

The farmer was horrified when he saw the filth and smelled the pungent reek of rotting corpses. He did not understand why the monk walked back and forth every day just to watch the birds feeding on the carcasses. And he was paying such close attention!

As the monk was about to leave, the farmer asked him, "Are these birds the witnesses you look for every day?" The monk affirmed that they were. The farmer then asked him, "Is it because you have committed some crime? Why do you need them to be witnesses?"

"These carcasses are so filthy, but my organs and body will be like them one day," the monk explained. "When I see this defilement, I remind myself: in my daily life, do I really want to continuously create bad karma for the sake of this body by committing evil acts? All bad deeds and their resulting karma arise from the body, and bodily actions in turn arise from the mind. Hence, I hope to control my mind and see clearly how impure my mind and body are, and thus eliminate the distractions and delusions in my mind."

"However, my delusions are difficult to remove and I frequently have thoughts that create bad karma," the monk continued. "Hence, I come here every day in the hope that these little birds will be my witnesses. I confess my thoughts to these birds every day, and I even tell them my thoughts from the previous day. I tell them that from now on I want to keep my mind tranquil and not let it be distracted by the beautiful things and lovely sounds in this world. I ask the birds to be my witnesses."

This is one method of doing spiritual cultivation. We are ordinary people. We may appreciate how defiled our bodies are when we see carcasses, and we may even reflect upon ourselves. However, after leaving the place and returning to our normal life, our minds tend to wander again. For example, the Buddha's teachings seem to make sense when we listen to them, and we feel that we have some appreciation for them. However, do we have the same appreciation towards the people and events we encounter in the next twenty-four hours? Can we concentrate on ourselves and let our minds truly stay in a quiet state of contemplation? We should therefore learn to manipulate our exterior circumstances with our minds, and not let our minds be carried away by our exterior circumstances.

For example, in the hospital we often see patients with rotting skin and festering flesh on their heads or abdomens. I wonder what feelings these images evoke in the minds of the volunteers who help the patients. Why are we so fussy about things for the sake of our defiled bodies? We should make good use of our bodies to do deeds that are of benefit to others. The more we can do so in our daily lives, the more merits we can accumulate. The more selfish we become, the more bad karma we create. May you be perceptive with your thoughts and constantly reflect on your true nature.

The Five Aggregates Are Empty

Sages have said, "The biggest problem for humans is the body." Most people crave material goods, prestige and power when they are healthy. However, do they know that in doing so they cause a lot of trouble and create bad karma?

During the Buddha's time, there was an elder by the name of Rolukan, a devout follower who respected the Buddha's teachings and all the monks and nuns. One morning, Rolukan came to pay his respects to the Buddha. He prostrated himself in front of the great teacher and then sat down. The Buddha asked, "Why are you here so early this morning?"

Rolukan replied, "I have a question for you: what should we do when we are suffering from the pain of illness?"

"Everyone knows the pain of illness," the Buddha replied, "but they don't know how to get rid of its cause."

"Then how can we eliminate the pain of illness?

"People often seek external pleasures to satisfy their cravings, but when their bodies fall ill their minds also become ill. This leads to great suffering. However, even if they are physically ill, they can be relieved immediately if their minds are not ill."

The elder listened to these words, and feeling that he understood a little of what the Buddha taught, he happily prostrated himself before the Buddha again and left. When he walked outside, he thought to himself, "Sariputra has learned so much from the Buddha. I wonder what his views on illness, life and death would be?" At this moment, he saw Sariputra meditating underneath a tree.

He walked towards the great disciple and prostrated himself in front of him.

"Sir, you look in very high spirits today," Sariputra observed. "Have you obtained some wise words from the Buddha?"

Rolukan affirmed that he had indeed, and Sariputra then asked him to elaborate. After hearing the elder's account of what he had learned, Sariputra posed a question: "What is needed to be physically ill and yet not be mentally affected?" Rolukan was at a loss as he realized that he had forgotten to ask the Buddha this question.

"Humans have afflictions caused by the Five Aggregates [form, sensation, perception, impulses, and consciousness]," Sariputra explained. "The body and everything we see around us are called 'form.' Having healthy bodies, many people are tempted by the things around them. They pursue things outside themselves and consequently experience many afflictions. With the passage of time, their bodies grow exhausted and become ill. They experience pain and suffering, and their daily lives become filled with fear of illness and death. In other words, their sensations, perceptions, impulses, and consciousness revolve entirely around pain and suffering. This is because they are so attached to the Five Aggregates. If they realize that the body has no inherently existing form, that all gains and pleasures are impermanent, and that aging, illness and death are natural occurrences, then physical ailments will no longer bring so much pain and suffering." Rolukan was delighted by Sariputra's words.

The message in this story is that our suffering arises from our attachments to the Five Aggregates.

A commissioner of our foundation once brought before me a young graduate student. The commissioner told me that he wanted my advice first before he made an important decision. I asked him to tell me his problem, to which he replied, "I am tortured by unrequited love and can't set myself free. Life is meaningless and I don't want to live anymore." The commissioner added, "He has attempted suicide several times, and he doesn't have the heart to pursue his degree anymore."

I asked him, "Why are you taking this relationship so seriously?"

"We've been going steady for many years."

"You've been going together for a long time, but how deep is your love? Here, show me... Bring it out and measure it for me."

He appeared to understand. "Yes, it can't be measured."

"Since this is the case," I went on, "why are you seeking death because of her? If this person is out of your life, will the sky fall down? Someone who deserves your love will never have a change of heart. Does one who changes her mind deserve your love? Why do you need to suffer and torture yourself because of her?"

"Now I understand," the young man said. "Master, are you suggesting that I complete my studies?"

"Yes, if you have the right views, your future is in your hands. You can use your wisdom to serve society. Why not transform the courage to take your own life into a commitment to serve others?"

He then answered that he understood what he should do, and he promised he would take his heart back and focus on his studies.

Is it worth it to harm ourselves because of afflictions caused by infatuated, selfish love? If we choose to be troubled by selfish love, we will surely hurt ourselves and others.

If we feel as if the world is falling apart merely because of some minor physical ailments and focus all our attention on our pain, our minds will also become ill. This is real suffering. Hence, I always say, "If physical ailments come, then endure them cheerfully." That is why I often remind people to maintain a healthy mind when they are physically ill. In conclusion, we should learn not be attached to our bodies and minds. If we do our best in our daily lives, then the true value of life will be revealed.

A Mind That Is Calm and Clear

The purpose of learning the Buddha's teachings is to clearly understand matters related to life and death, where we came from and where we will go after we die. This is not easy. However, the Buddha has wisely guided us by instructing us on the first step—calming the mind. If the mind is calm, the world around us will be clear and we can then thoroughly reflect on our true selves and understand how we are living at the present moment. If we can have open minds and take everything as being in the normal run of events, we will naturally be at ease and not be attached to life and death.

There was a time when the Buddha and his disciples were living at the Abode of the Bamboo Grove in Rajagrha. Because there were so many disciples, a group of them, led by Sariputra, lived at Vulture Peak Mountain. Sariputra was known to be the wisest among all the Buddha's disciples, and the other monks approached him if they had questions.

One day, Mahakusula was meditating when these questions came to him: "How was I born? Why is there life, death, and ignorance in human life?"

Mahakusula could not answer these questions. He rose from his meditation seat, walked over to Sariputra's room, and spoke respectfully to him. "Respected one, I have some questions. The Buddha frequently says that living beings arise out of a confluence of ignorance. Where is ignorance located? Where does it come from? How do we free ourselves from ignorance?"

"Ignorance comes from incomprehension," Sariputra replied. "In fact, it arises from not comprehending that form, sensation, perception, impulses, and consciousness have no real, inherent existence. It arises because we do not mindfully reflect upon the fact that the 'form' aggregate permeates human existence—everything that we see is form that arises and disappears. Because we do not understand why things come and go, we frequently become attached to things. This is ignorance. In addition, we do not understand the aggregate of 'sensation,' which arises in our hearts. Whatever we see, hear, or come in touch with gives rise to sensations. Those that are pleasant give rise to joy; those that are unpleasant give rise to anger. If we do not understand that sensation has no real, inherent existence, afflictions arise. This is also called ignorance."

Sariputra continued: "Upon experiencing sensation, ordinary people have their own perceptions or ways of thinking. If there is attachment even after the event has come to pass, this is called ignorance. Why is there 'impulse' associated with life and death? This, too, comes from attachment. We use our 'consciousness' to experience external events and commit actions that we later regret. This is called ignorance. If we cannot thoroughly understand the Five Aggregates, there will be doubts in our minds. This is also called ignorance."

How can we thoroughly comprehend Sariputra's very abstract logic on the Five Aggregates? It depends on how diligent we are.

For example, consider the sand, rocks, grass, and trees on earth, and even our bodies. All these are included in the 'form' aggregate. Why does a single stalk of grass sprout from the earth? This is because of the combination of the grass seed, soil, water, sunlight and air. All these conditions must continue to exist for the grass to continue growing. However, after the grass has grown for a period of time, it will turn yellow and wilt. This is change from "impulse"— there is continuous arising, change and extinction.

Human life is like that. We have to go through the stages of infancy, childhood, adolescence, middle age and old age. How do we grow from one stage to another? In my opinion, it is hard for us to thoroughly understand our own bodies. It is also difficult to thoroughly understand the aggregate of 'consciousness' that constantly comes and goes, or understand our own thinking and sensations.

In the hospital, we see patients with different ailments and their different perspectives towards life. Some people are fearful of death and think about the terror of death whenever they are ill. Hence, some people do not really die from illnesses, but from the fear of death—their terror and worry exacerbate their ailments. On the other hand some people are optimistic, and their chances of recovery are better.

There was a patient suffering from cirrhosis of the liver. He expressed his intention to donate his body after his death to the Tzu Chi College of Medicine for anatomy classes. He said that in his whole life he had never made any contributions to society, and his donation of his impermanent, decaying body after his death was the least he could do.

Such an optimistic person can be said to have transcended his attachment to the 'form' aggregate and to life and death. Whether he has a clear understanding of the aggregates of sensation, perception, impulse and consciousness is really unimportant. Once the initial step of comprehending and being less attached to the form aggregate has been taken, the rest is easy. Therefore, we must reflect on ourselves. If our minds can calm down, ignorance will not be able to dominate us.

Sand of the Ganges

I recall that about twenty years ago, Venerable Master Tung Chu visited the Abode of Still Thoughts and was deeply impressed with the place where we practice the Buddha's teachings. He felt that our living environment was simple, elegant, and well suited to our activities. Once when I was in Taipei, I had the opportunity to visit the master. He was delighted to see me. From an alcove, he carefully took out a small object wrapped in red cloth. He said, "Dear Master, I'm giving you a very special treat—I'm sharing with you something I brought back from India."

He cautiously untied the string around the object and removed the red cloth, layer by layer. He took out a small, clean bottle and said, "I can only give you a little bit..." I asked, "Venerable One, what is it?" He replied, "People who visit the Ganges River always take some sand back with them. This is sand that the Buddha once walked on. It is very precious indeed."

I looked carefully at the sparkling sand that was as fine as flour. Upon my return to the Abode in eastern Taiwan, I respectfully placed this sacred relic on the shrine in the library.

I once went to visit some needy people in Chihsingtan, a village located not too far away from the Pacific Ocean. The beach sparkled in the sunlight, just like the Ganges River sand! However, the sand here has less value: people who obviously did not value the sand were leading their water buffaloes on it. It is the same sand on the same earth. However, its value differs depending on our mindset.

After I had made that visit, I returned to the Abode and took down the Ganges River sand from the shrine. There is so much sand on earth. Why did I choose to put this little bit of sand from the Ganges River on my shrine? Why was I treating the two types of sand so differently? After a while, I realized that the difference lay in Master Tung Chu's way of thinking. He had brought the sand back from distant India, and he had emphasized, "Only to you would I give a little of this sand." These words had such great impact on me. Furthermore, his kindness was most valuable. Because of his kindness, I had put the sand on the shrine. The master felt that the Ganges River sand bore the traces of the Buddha's footprints, and so he was particularly respectful towards it. These thoughts arose from respect. Isn't it true that mind alone creates everything?

During the Buddha's time, his disciple Kumalakasyapa was in a nearby village cultivating himself and promoting the Buddha's teachings. One day, a wealthy elder came to consult him. "Holy man, I frequently hear you teach us that upon death a person's consciousness will follow his good or bad karma and rise to heaven or descend to hell. This sounds logical, but how would you prove it? You also said that mind alone creates everything, but what is this mind? What is its function and what does it look like?"

"Sir, let me give you an example," Kumalakasyapa replied. "Suppose a person committed a felony and the king sentenced him to death. Do you think the king will grant a request by his family members to allow him to go home to visit his relatives?"

The elder replied, "How can this be possible? Since he is to face the gallows soon, how can he go home?"

Kumalakasyapa followed with this question: "Using the same logic, if a person has descended to hell for an infinite time because of his bad karma, how can he possibly return to the human world to provide evidence?"

The elder asked another question: "How about the people who ascend to heaven? Can't they come back?"

"Let me give you another example. If a person dreams that he is having a joyous reunion with his relatives, will his relatives be able to feel it?"

"Only the dreamer can feel it, but not others."

"It is the same logic. All of us have our own good and bad karma that only we ourselves, not others, experience. Although there is no direct evidence, remember that faith is the source of the Right Path and mother of all merits."

The wife of a wealthy entrepreneur once told me, "My brother-in-law does not believe in the law of cause and effect. I tried to get him to go to Tzu Chi activities, but he said, 'All of you say that good deeds beget good outcomes, and that there is the law of cause and effect. Show me some proof.' I don't know how to convince him on this matter."

I answered: "It's hard to provide evidence on reincarnation in the Six Realms of heaven, human, asura, animal, hungry ghost and hell. We have to perceive it with our minds. If you do not have sincere belief, or if you are unwilling to comprehend this in your heart, then asking someone else for proof is like an ignorant man sleepwalking—he will never see the Path."

"But he believes in *feng shui* [geomancy]," the woman added. "Some people said that his father's burial site was wrong, and so he spent a lot of money to have it moved."

How ironic! It was not that he had no belief—he was just superstitious.

We need to be logical when learning Buddhism. Try using the real events which happen in our daily lives as examples to differentiate right from wrong. In reality, the most fearful thing is when our minds and actions go astray—this is the most genuine example of cause and effect. In understanding the law of cause and effect, it is important to place emphasis on our current actions rather than our karmic consequences. This is because cause and effect really depend on how we behave at this very moment.

Therefore, do not think that if things are not going well, it is because there is something wrong with your ancestors' feng shui. Why create such afflictions for ourselves, when the denizens of this world and those of the nether world go their separate ways? The purpose of learning the Buddha's teachings is to increase our wisdom. It is not to create unnecessary pressures for others, or to make others do things according to the way we want out of fear. True Buddhism can bring joy to us and motivate us to walk on the Path of the Bodhisattvas. It is not about strange metaphysical stuff that induces fear in us. In sum, a true Buddhist should have right views without superstitions.

Three Corn Cakes

Doing charity is like digging a well: once the well has been dug, the water will flow continuously. The problem is that we do not know how to dig the well. Giving alms is not a specialty of the wealthy—all people who so desire can give alms. The Buddha said that the most meritorious giving is that which is motivated by the greatest joy and the greatest sincerity.

There was a story about the Buddha when he and his disciples were at Rajagrha. At that time there were many religions in India, and a common concept then was that people who were spiritually cultivated were entitled to receive offerings and that the giver would receive merits by doing so. As a result, all practitioners regardless of their religion (e.g., Hinduism, Brahmanism) received offerings from other people.

After the Buddha's enlightenment, many people of high status frequently invited the Buddha and his disciples to lavish meals. But he felt that he should let the masses have the opportunity to get in touch with his teachings and to personally make offerings to accumulate merits. Therefore, he announced, "Henceforth, everyone, regardless of wealth and social status, can make offerings and gain merits."

One day, some people on the streets of Rajagrha were discussing how they should make offerings to the Buddha, now that he had returned to this place. One of them was a poor laborer who, like the rest, very much wanted to make offerings to the Buddha. However, when he returned home, he found that his rice jar was empty. He was troubled, not knowing what he could possibly offer to the Buddha. He searched for a while, but all he found was some slightly discolored corn flour that already smelled moldy. He wasn't sure what to do, but decided that since this was all he had, he would make the best use of it. He added water to the corn flour and made it into corn cakes. He then wrapped them with walnut leaves and baked them. Altogether, he made three corn cakes, which were all he could make with the available corn flour.

With the utmost sincerity, he took these three corn cakes to the gathering place. At the scheduled time, the Buddha and his disciples arrived. All the laypeople had their bowls filled with delicious food. They held their bowls high, hoping that the Buddha would personally take the food from their bowls.

The Buddha observed that among these people, one held up some food wrapped in leaves, but he immediately lowered his offering and his head when he saw the Buddha. The poor man was thinking that everybody else's offerings were so substantial, whereas his own was too shabby to offer to the Buddha. Ashamed, he lowered his hands with the corn cakes.

But the Buddha walked towards him, and lovingly asked him, "Don't you want to make an offering?" The poor man was very touched, and offered his corn cakes to the Buddha. With tears in his eyes, this poor man wondered how, with so much delicious food around, the Buddha could accept his offering.

At this time, many people were talking about the whole incident and gazing at the lucky man. They asked him, "What did you offer the Buddha?" The poor man murmured, "Some corn cakes made from flour that was about to turn bad."

When they heard what he said, people criticized him in their hearts for offering the venerable Buddha such shabby fare.

Word spread around even to the king and ministers. They quickly rushed over and found the Buddha eating the cakes with relish. They all felt that the merits of the poor man must have been very great.

Some people tried to give money to the poor man, begging him to let them participate in the offering and to let them share some of his merits. The poor man remarked, "I just offered some poor food to the Buddha. What merits do I have to share with you?" But the others said, "If you accept our money, it means that we are also participating in the offering that you made to the Buddha. We will then certainly share some of your merits."

The poor man was unsure. Puzzled, he went to the Buddha. "Oh Venerable One, many people want to offer me money so that I can share my merits with them. Is that possible?"

The Buddha replied, "Yes, you can accept their money."

"How can I transfer my merits to them?"

"You will make them happy by taking their money. This joy itself is a merit."

Yes, if we can make others joyful, that is a merit. Tzu Chi has been walking its path since 1966. We have used our utmost sincerity in serving others, and people have also used their utmost sincerity and gratitude in helping and donating to us. Thus, as I always say, Tzu Chi is a world of gratitude and Great Love, a world where the cycle of gratitude and love will come full circle. We use what people give to do social work and to help needy people in Taiwan and around the world. We bring love together and use it to benefit the whole world.

Tzu Chi people can now be found throughout the world. Whether it is charity, medical care, educational or cultural work, Tzu Chi people do it with great joy. We can say that the seeds of love and the power of love have been transmitted to every corner of the world. May this love bear fruit in every corner of this world, and may everyone enjoy the fruits of peace and joy.

The Color of Life

Being a bodhisattva is really not difficult. Anyone who wants to can become a living bodhisattva in the human world. The Buddha said, "If the mind is pure, the land is pure." A single good thought can permeate the ten dharma-worlds. Do you want to attain buddhahood and walk on the Path of the Bodhisattvas, or would you rather be just an ordinary person or even be reborn in the three Lower Realms of the animals, hungry ghosts or hell? All this depends on a single thought!

"The mind, the Buddha, and all living beings—there is no difference among these three." The moment you generate a thought of compassion, you have the Buddha's mind—at that moment, you are the Buddha. When you cannot bear to see others suffer and you try your best to help them, you are a bodhisattva. When you turn away from the sufferings of others and only care for yourself, you are being selfish and are not following the Buddha's teachings. The Buddha told his followers, "If you want to make yourself remarkable, you must first help make the people around you remarkable." This is the spirit of a bodhisattva.

There are so many people in this world, but how many will actually aspire to become bodhisattvas? In reality, it is not difficult to become a bodhisattva; it is just that the conditions are not right for some people to participate in such endeavors. The sutras say, "It is difficult for the rich to learn the way of enlightenment." This is because the rich do not have an appropriate environment to do so. Every day they lead luxurious lives. They pursue lives of luxury, fame and fortune.

What meaning is there in such pursuits? Some people say, "This person is rich and his life is so interesting and colorful." However, I think that such a life is quite meaningless: he is waiting for his next meal even though he has just eaten; he wants more even though he has the best money can buy; he has nothing better to do than sleep even though he is not tired. What glory is there in a life that revolves around good food, sleep and enjoyment?

If one can truly be engaged in society and seek to understand the sources of human pain and suffering, one will understand that life is like a stage. Some people are very steady and composed on stage. They play their roles well and know what scripts they have to act. Such people have a stable and fulfilling life because they are in control of where they want to go. They are not lost; they are fully aware of their duty to society.

For example Mr. Wen, a high-ranking military officer who had just retired from the army, had led a glorious and comfortable life. But once he retired, he thought he should rest and withdraw from everything. Every day he read the newspaper, chatted with others, or found ways to keep fit. His life had become so limited that he expected to be fed and served. With the passing of time, his relationship with his wife deteriorated. Such a life is quite meaningless, no matter how long and healthy it might be.

However, after he joined Tzu Chi, his life changed. He began to be more mindful and make the best of his life. He learned to treat his wife well and help her with the housework, and they began a new phase of companionship in their old age. I believe that this kind of family life was more meaningful and harmonious than the one they experienced when they were younger.

There was another old lady who was at first unhappy with her daughter-in-law for engaging in Tzu Chi activities. "You can't even finish your own work," she thought. "Why bother to get involved in other people's business? Why eat your own food but do the work of others?" With such a narrow, self-centered perspective of life, one can never be happy. When in-laws bicker over trifles, they will not be able to get along well with each other.

Fortunately, this daughter-in-law patiently kept trying to make her mother-in-law understand what she was doing. She also took her sisters-in-law along with her to do volunteer work. Now, this mother-in-law knows the joy of helping others, and she is grateful to her daughter-in-law for bringing the whole family into Tzu Chi. They have something in common to talk about every day, and they are able to coordinate their work very well. This is indeed a case where harmony has brought family bliss.

When family members can talk about things they have in common and share the same altruistic commitment, they are indeed happy. The sages said, "First cultivate yourself, then manage your family, go on to rule the nation, and finally bring peace to the world." If every family is blissful, society will be harmonious. Tzu Chi is one big family working to bring harmony to society and praying that the world will be free of disasters. We still have a long way to go. We need more people to work wholeheartedly together on our shared goals—to create a harmonious society and a world without disasters.

A Diamond-Like Life

Life is short. When we deduct the time spent in ignorance during childhood and the time spent on receiving an education, we realize that there is very little time left for us to serve society.

The first few decades of life are meant to build a good foundation so that we can later contribute to society. How long can we contribute? Just when we begin to feel that we are making useful contributions, we find we are getting old. The time we can devote to helping others is indeed short. People who realize this will value their time and make the best of every minute and second to create a meaningful life.

A middle-aged man got drunk and started a fight with seven others. He had boasted to his friends that he was a hero who could single-handedly battle against seven others. Although the others were hurt, his own injuries were not slight either. But what hurt him the most was his anger—he often could not get along well with others, and had frequently been involved in lawsuits for attacking others. Even after a court settlement, the animosity in his heart (and that of others) was difficult to overcome. He had to be constantly looking over his shoulder in case others sought revenge. Because of his lack of understanding of the meaning of life he hurt himself, brought sorrow and anxiety to his family, and brought discord to others. This meaningless and pathetic kind of lifestyle is harmful to society.

Hospital volunteers frequently witness and learn from such cases. These cases are important pragmatic lessons in life, and they encourage us to contemplate and reflect. I believe that these salient lessons are deeply imprinted on our minds. Once we learn these lessons, we must ensure that we use them well in our daily lives.

Having seen many such cases, one young volunteer realized how fortunate his life had been. His mother, a Tzu Chi commissioner, had filled their home with love and wisdom, but he had become used to it and did not think it was anything special. It is like a person breathing: humans need oxygen to live, but in a well-ventilated space we may not feel any urgent need for oxygen to stay healthy and alive. Or it is like a fish swimming in water: the fish cannot survive outside water, but while it is immersed in water it does not feel how precious the water is. Similarly, things that are habitual become natural. Things that are generally most important are easily taken for granted. However, this is not a bad situation, as it is a normal response to a healthy lifestyle.

We have to hold in our minds whatever lessons we learn from the cases we are exposed to. We have to constantly remind ourselves of these lessons till they become part of our lives and are no longer unusual or abnormal. Then, we can claim that we have succeeded. This is analogous to what the Buddha said: "Doing spiritual cultivation to the extent that you do not realize you are doing it is real cultivation." If we only talk about doing our spiritual cultivation, that is not real cultivation. But if we practice till it becomes a normal part of life, then that is real cultivation.

Let me give you another example. Why do patients place so much trust in the volunteers at our hospitals? Because the volunteers consistently take care of these patients and develop a good relationship with them. But are these volunteers friendly and helpful only when they wear the Tzu Chi volunteer vests? We should practice the volunteer spirit every day, until it becomes as natural to us as the air we breath.

If we can give others peace of mind or a shoulder to lean on, then we have truly lived meaningful lives. This is a measure of a meaningful life. The length of our lives is not important; what is important is how much we have benefited others.

Time flies by. Let us treat time like a precious diamond and not like dirt. This is respecting our lives. It goes beyond caring for others when they are ill and helping others when they are in trouble. Respect for our lives means that we make proper use of our time, that we value our time and use it appropriately in our work. We will gain the respect of others if our lives are meaningful. We should always be mindful and create a life that will shine like a diamond.

Loving Oneself and Others

The Buddha came to the world to save all living beings, and we humans are the ones who suffer because our minds are full of greed, anger, delusion, arrogance and doubt. These five afflictions will not only hurt our physical bodies, but will tarnish our wisdom as well.

Therefore, I often say, "It is not just other living beings that feel affliction and suffering—it is often us." Thus, we have to solve our own problems before we can help solve the problems of others. We have to make ourselves happy before we can make others happy. We have to remove our own afflictions before we can remove the afflictions of others. This is called compassion.

Just see how many people nowadays hurt themselves and others because of these five afflictions. They feel bad about the things they have done. Although they might not yet have been caught, they cannot escape the reproach of their own conscience. They are truly suffering beings. Yet they have only themselves to blame.

Some people do not hurt others but themselves. Nowadays, many people do silly things and then try to commit suicide by all kinds of methods, such as jumping off high-rises or plunging into the sea. Even if they survive the attempt, they are sometimes so severely injured that they cannot live a normal life. In the hospital, we frequently see people who have caused themselves grievous harm and life-long regret because of a psychological problem or a moment of weakness. This is affliction and suffering of the mind and spirit.

Some people want to torture or punish others by hurting themselves physically. This is a very disturbed mindset that will not only drag them into misery, but bring agony to their family members and loved ones as well. Overall, much of the pain and suffering of mankind arise because people cannot transcend the sources of their afflictions. They cannot deal with one another with understanding, accommodation or gratitude, let alone contentment.

Our minds will be magnanimous if we can always bear contentment, gratitude, understanding and accommodation in mind. We can be joyful when we are content with what we have. We should try to be understanding and grateful in our dealings with others. We should be accommodating and tolerant towards the shortcomings of other people. Once our minds are open, nothing will bother us.

Some people say, "I am a Buddhist and I want to redeem all living beings from their suffering." However, they frequently forget about themselves. Although they want to give love, they do not love themselves.

To love oneself does not mean to put everything aside, sit back and rest on one's laurels. "We do not have the right to own our bodies; we only have the right to use them." Since we have come to this earth, we should make the best use of our bodies. Otherwise, we are merely spending a great deal of time every day taking care of this body—feeding it when it is hungry, washing it when it is sweaty, resting it when it gets tired. How much time do we spend on our bodies? How much friction and discord do we cause to "protect" our bodies? If we don't make the best use of our bodies, it will be a waste. Thus, loving ourselves does not mean that we don't use our bodies. Rather, it means that we should use them properly.

To use our bodies well, we have to maintain them in the best condition they can be. The most important aspect is to maintain a healthy mind. This is because everything we say and do arises from the mind. If thoughts do not arise, the body will not create karma, either good or bad. Greed, anger, delusion, arrogance and doubt are the major obstacles that block our wisdom. Hence, we must use our minds to overcome and eliminate these five mental impediments.

Most people are sometimes able to calm the minds of others, but few can truly calm their own minds. Many people know how to help others, but they forget about their own afflicted minds. Just think about it—does the phrase "suffering living beings" refer only to others? We should not just ask all the buddhas and bodhisattvas to bless us and help remove our pain and suffering. Instead we should try to acquire compassion and the wisdom to transcend our hardships.

The Buddha appeared in this world to help us learn a lesson: he learned by watching other people how to attain enlightenment for himself. He was reminded by others that no matter how fortunate he was, he could not escape from the suffering of birth, aging, illness, death, parting from loved ones, encountering those he disliked, and the Five Aggregates of form, sensation, perception, impulse and consciousness. The Buddha let go of everything and sought the truth of the universe. On his way to attain enlightenment, he began his quest for the truth as an ordinary person and learned step by step to give unselfishly. He could mindfully investigate all the suffering that people endured and then overcome the barriers in his own mind, thereby attaining enlightenment.

Hence, the Buddha's teachings came from his understanding of his own experiences and efforts. Similarly, the Tzu Chi way has been slowly paved inch by inch through the personal participation of many individuals. Has the road been completely paved? Not yet. I still need everyone to work with me to pave the road ahead. The journey is still long and arduous and the goal is still far ahead. To construct a road, we need people to clear away all the obstacles and pave the road, and we need people to plant trees to provide shade for travelers. Those who get personally involved in this process will benefit more and have a stronger sense of accomplishment than those who do not. Through actual practice, we can increase our compassion and wisdom and remove our doubts.

Hence, everyone should thoroughly understand this: we must not merely ask for the blessings of the bodhisattvas. Instead, we should seek to increase our wisdom to help others whenever possible and, more importantly, to learn how to save ourselves.

Four Treasures in Life

Deeds of love should not be performed alone. We should also motivate others to join us in doing the same. Furthermore, these acts should not be done only for a moment—they should be done throughout our lives. No one should think that they are old and useless. Rather, once we get on in age, we should seize every opportunity to do more good deeds and accumulate more merits.

An old lady and her daughter-in-law came to visit me. During our conversation, the old lady told me, "Master, the older I get, the busier I get. My daughter-in-law always wakes up late, while my son has to get to work and my grandchildren have to go to school. Since she doesn't get up to prepare breakfast, I have to do so. I'm really getting busier as I get older." The daughter-in-law sat on one side and said, "Mother, you're getting old, so I should let you have the chance to do some exercise."

"Did you hear that?" I asked the mother-in-law. "She has no bad intentions. She wants to let you get up earlier to exercise. We're getting old. If we don't do any work now, there won't be many more opportunities for us. So we should be grateful we can still do something." These words were meant to console and encourage the old lady.

To the daughter-in-law, I said, "A daughter-in-law should show concern and respect to her elders. You are the model for your children. They will learn from how you treat your in-laws, so you should be a good role model for them. Furthermore, your parents and in-laws are true living buddhas. You must respect your elders, treat them with filial piety, and make them happy. When you manage your family with love and filial piety, merits and bliss will naturally accumulate."

I have often said that we would have a blissful life if we could "sleep in peace, eat with happiness, laugh with joy, and work in good health." We often pray for a peaceful society and fair weather. If society is harmonious and peaceful, we will be able to sleep tight every night without worrying about floods or other natural disasters, or about burglars breaking into our houses.

We must have confidence. If all of us have good intentions to do good deeds and fulfill our duties, we can slowly influence society. If everyone has a good heart and good thoughts, society will be peaceful and harmonious. Thus, if we are at peace and have faith in others, we can "sleep in peace."

If everyone acts to the best of his or her means, then each occupation in our society will flourish: the husband will focus on his career, the children will study hard, and the housewife will perform her duties well. All the family members will even be able to engage in charity work together. At night, when they all come home for dinner, they will have common themes to talk about over the dinner table. The whole family will be together and happily enjoy each other's company. Thus, they can "eat with happiness."

When our minds have no afflictions, we will constantly do good for others with no intention to harm them. Our relationships with others will then be harmonious. We have to be open-minded and appreciate the viewpoints of others. We should be accommodating and understanding when faced with disputes. We must be content with what we have and always be grateful to others. If we keep these four treasures in mind, we will have no afflictions. Without afflictions, we will be joyful in our dealings with people or events. We will smile sincerely, not wryly, from the bottom of our hearts. This is to "laugh with joy."

People often lament that they are old and useless. It doesn't matter that we are old. What is important is to be healthy and willing to work. Such people are most fortunate. Some people may not have had the opportunity to perform loving acts when they were young. Now that their children have grown up and they do not need to worry about their financial situation, they can mindfully do good deeds in the latter half of their lives. For example, our Tzu Chi Foundation currently has many ongoing projects, such as erecting hospitals and rebuilding schools toppled in the great earthquake of September 1999. Every handful of sand, every brick, and every steel rod goes into the construction of buildings that will help people. To be able to engage as fully as one can in such activities by donating money or labor is to accumulate merits. This is to "work in good health."

If all of us sincerely use our love to engage in the four Tzu Chi missions of charity, medical care, education and cultural activities, we can create a great path together.

Hence, we must persevere and avoid improper deeds, ill words and evil thoughts. We should not demand that others accommodate us; rather, we must train ourselves to accommodate others. We have to learn how to love others and work together, for in unity there is great strength. Let us make proper use of our lives and our abilities. We must not think about personal benefits when dealing with events or people around us. Instead, we must try to perform our duties well and maintain a tranquil mind that is free from worries at all times.

Repaying the Kindness of Others

A Tzu Chi member who owned a factory in South Africa emigrated from Taiwan to England. One day, he called me from England and told me he might shut down the plant in South Africa and return to Taiwan. I asked him why, because I knew that several thousand workers depended on their jobs there. He then told me he had no other choice, since the situation in South Africa was unstable and there was a lot of looting and arson.

I knew he had emigrated and set up his plant in South Africa because he had felt that the situation in Taiwan was unstable. I reminded him that all people come to earth with their past karma. If his karma led him into situations of instability and unrest, he could not escape from it; if he did not have this karma, he would never experience such problems. I advised him that since he had set up his factory in South Africa, he should repay that country for what he had gained from it. Taiwanese are not respected overseas because they are seen as exploiting the resources and cheap labor of the country in which they set up their factories and keeping the revenues for themselves. Local people in these countries contribute their labor but do not get much in return. As a result, they continue to lead a poor life. A life of poverty often gives rise to thoughts of robbery and stealing. The larger the gap between the rich and poor, the more likely the poor will try to get even with the rich. I told this person that he should change his mode of operation by repaying the local society with the profits he had gained. He would then earn respect.

I told him the following true story: In 1996, there was unrest amongst African-Americans in Los Angeles. A Tzu Chi member who had immigrated to the United States from southern Taiwan was out driving at the time. When she approached the city, several African-Americans suddenly surrounded her car and demanded in an unfriendly tone, "Which country are you from—Korea, Japan or China?" People from these countries look pretty much the same to many Americans.

This Tzu Chi member was very frightened, and answered them bluntly, "I'm a Chinese from Taiwan." When they heard this, their attitudes changed. Surprisingly, they even smiled at her and said, "Don't drive any further. It's dangerous. You should take another route." The poor woman was puzzled why their attitude should change so drastically when they heard that she was from Taiwan. When she got home, she asked her African-American maid for her views on this incident. She replied, "When the blacks stirred up unrest in that area, they had a common understanding— protect the Taiwanese and rob the Koreans and Japanese." The woman curiously asked about the reason behind this strange attitude. The maid replied, "Because the Tzu Chi people from Taiwan have been very kind to us. They provide scholarships for our children, care about our livelihood, and frequently help us." The woman asked further, "Which organization did you just mention?" The maid confirmed it was Tzu Chi. The member was very encouraged by what she had heard and quickly phoned another Tzu Chi member in Taiwan to share this interesting episode and to express her gratitude to Tzu Chi.

After hearing this story, the member who set up the factory in South Africa was inspired and said, "Master, now I know what to do." He then flew from England to South Africa, gathered all his plant's supervisors and announced that he would not shut down the plant. He further asked them to show more concern for the welfare of the black employees because, just as Master Cheng Yen had said, "We need to contribute to others before we can earn their respect."

He also brought together many Taiwanese businessmen in South Africa to look after the welfare of the blacks. During that time, although there was still frequent looting, Tzu Chi members bravely entered the black districts with carloads of medicine, food and daily necessities for distribution to the poor. They have been doing this continuously for five years. Because Tzu Chi people offered their sincere concern, their black friends were also very grateful to them.

Tzu Chi's Great Love is an altruism that transcends the boundaries of nationality, religion and race. As long as we are willing to give, we will surely be rewarded with the same amount of kindness. Let's start from our own neighborhood and fill every corner with love. We will then be assured of the day when society will be harmonious and there will be no disasters in the world.

Put Our Love into Action

The earthquake that struck Taiwan on September 21, 1999, broke my heart. No words can express my sorrow. I pray that all who died during this catastrophe can rest in peace and, as they wished, be reborn as humans. I also sincerely bless all the victims who suffered injuries and the victims' relatives who went through such great shock. I hope they can soon recover from their pain and settle back to their normal lives.

I am very grateful to Tzu Chi members from all over Taiwan who rushed to the disaster areas to provide help and offer food to victims on a twenty-four-hour basis. As long as rescuers worked in the disaster areas, Tzu Chi members stayed on! Many Tzu Cheng Faith Corps members also engaged in rescue missions and risked their lives to take food to the disaster areas, despite the fact that many roads and bridges were inaccessible and there were still many aftershocks. Their fearless determination truly moved me.

I was very worried about the homeless survivors. What would they do if it rained? Therefore we purchased a considerable number of tents and rushed them to the disaster areas. Through Tzu Chi members all over the island, we sent the word out that we would freely supply without limit all daily necessities to survivors of the earthquake. As a result, Tzu Chi members in the north and south sped off on the highways with carloads of supplies. When it was dark or the roads were blocked, they tried all different ways to overcome these obstacles. I was very grateful but very worried for them. But I was even more worried about how to save victims still trapped in the rubble.

My appreciation goes to Tzu Chi Hospital's superintendent, vice superintendent and other hospital workers, who
immediately set up a medical rescue team. On the very afternoon of the earthquake, forty of these team members headed
off to Taiwan's central area, where the earthquake struck,
and immediately got to work without resting. I am also
grateful to the Tzu Chi International Medical Association. At
ten that morning, TIMA members gathered in Taichung and
from there went out in seven teams to the most severely
damaged areas. Together with the medical rescue team, I
believe they brought much relief to the victims.

After the earthquake, someone asked, "How long will
Tzu Chi help the victims?" I replied, "Until the work is finished." For twenty-four hours a day, we worked non-stop to
provide necessary emergency relief supplies and services to
victims and rescue workers. Every Tzu Chi member in the
country was on one of three shifts twenty-four hours a day,
and provided whatever was needed. We would continue to
work with the survivors for a long time to come, so it was
really difficult to tell exactly when our efforts would end. My
heart ached whenever I thought about the deceased. May
they rest in peace. May the wounded quickly recover from
their injuries and shock, and may bereaved relatives recover
from their sorrow. The path that survivors and their families
must traverse is very long and arduous, but we will accompany them along the way.

I recall that earlier, when we launched a fund-raising cam-
paign for earthquake victims in Turkey [which had a major
earthquake just a month before the one in Taiwan], someone
angrily pointed his finger right in the face of one commis-

sioner and demanded: "Tell me, where is Turkey? Where is the disaster? Why are you saving Turkey instead of Taiwan?" I felt a stabbing pain in my heart when I heard such criticism. I couldn't figure out why people wanted to save Taiwan. Actually, to have to be saved is not something we would look forward to, since that would mean that there had been some disaster that we had to be saved from. Now a calamity really has struck and, just as they said, we have to save Taiwan. That is why I always say, "We should resolve to be people who can save others."

Needing to be saved is a situation out of the victim's control. Hence, I frequently say that we should aspire to be people who can save others and never curse ourselves by asking "Why not save Taiwan?" Needing to be saved is truly a tragic affair.

On the afternoon of the earthquake in Taiwan, a Japanese rescue team brought specially trained dogs to search for survivors. They were followed by rescue teams from Singapore, Russia, Germany, the United States, Britain, Switzerland, Turkey and Mexico. Such manifestations of humanitarian concern brought much warmth to our society.

Chungliao District in Nantou County was severely hit by the earthquake, and the authorities asked for all the resources that could be provided. They needed all sorts of relief supplies urgently. It was heartbreaking to hear this! I remember that after the earthquake in Turkey, our rescue volunteers asked victims there what they needed. They replied, "Anything! We can't choose." Since we had to supply so much at such short notice, it was apparent that the victims did not have the option to choose what they wanted.

In the aftermath of the disaster, I immediately reminded our commissioners in Taipei that the thing the victims needed most urgently was cash, because the victims had not carried anything with them in their rush to escape. Relief payments needed to be distributed at once, so that the victims could go buy some necessities. The commissioners told me they had already given out all the cash they had at home, but it was still not enough. I said, "We can withdraw money from the banks." They told me all the banks were shut down due to widespread power failure, and so they could not withdraw any money.

What made matters worse was that there was nowhere to buy supplies because many stores in Taipei and Taichung were closed. I immediately instructed our staff members to withdraw NT$20 million [US$667,000] from the banks in Hualien and distribute the money to victims in Taipei, Taichung and other devastated areas so that they could at least buy some emergency supplies locally. Later, I asked the commissioners if there was enough money. Their answer was negative. I told them not to worry about it, I would think of other ways to get cash for the victims. Tzu Chi spent roughly NT$160 million [US$5.2 million] on relief payments in the first three days after the temblor. Each household in the disaster areas received NT$5,000 [US$161]. As for those that had lost family members, the foundation distributed NT$20,000 [US$645] for each deceased person.

The rescue operation for this great catastrophe involved practically all the Tzu Chi members in Taiwan, including hundreds and thousands of commissioners, Tzu Cheng Faith Corps members, and volunteers. We are grateful to the

Chinese Petroleum Corporation for its loan of a helicopter, which allowed us to distribute supplies to victims in remote areas not easily accessible by ordinary vehicles. The helicopter also enabled us to conduct surveillance to assess if there were other areas in Nantou that needed assistance. The Police Administration in Taipei also dispatched a helicopter to distribute supplies for us. These helicopters started off from Taipei, flew to Taichung to pick up rescue team members and supplies, and then transported them to the disaster areas. Fortunately a group of jeep enthusiasts, the "Camel Jeep Troop," pitched in to help us and drive our volunteers around. Several years ago they met Tzu Chi medical personnel who were conducting free clinics in remote mountain areas. Moved by their selfless assistance to the poor, they promised they would help Tzu Chi whenever possible. They had first-rate communications equipment, which they put at our disposal. With their assistance we were able to gather information on disaster areas, and we could contact support people in Taipei and other counties and tell them what things they should bring along and where they should go. We tried to purchase all the emergency supplies that we needed. Later, many donors continued to offer these supplies, and we tried our best to sort them and distribute them to victims.

It is hard to believe that at the end of the century, Taiwan was devastated by such a major disaster. This earthquake claimed over two thousand precious lives and left us feeling pained and helpless. Fortunately, some areas were unaffected; residents there were frightened but not physically harmed, which was a relief and a matter for rejoicing. However, everyone should be on the alert and love should never leave our hearts. May everyone contribute their efforts or money and sincerely set out to help our fellow victims who need help.

Protecting Our Global Village

The earthquake that ravaged Taiwan on September 21, 1999, was one of the worst disasters to have ever struck Taiwan. After that incident, I felt sad and very concerned about the situation in the disaster areas. What I saw on television every day was so tragic that I could not bear to watch the scenes, yet I could not bear to turn a blind eye and ignore what was happening. It is simply beyond my ability to describe that feeling of sadness. It was like the situation I found myself in over forty years ago when my father passed away—I wanted to cry, but no tears would flow.

The world is like a global village. When other countries were experiencing disasters, we tried our best to help them solve their problems; now Taiwan in turn has received concern and aid from humanitarian organizations in other countries. I had mixed feelings when I saw this, since on the one hand I felt grateful for their help, but on the other wished we had not been devastated by the earthquake. I have often said that we who are born in this world are all brothers and sisters, even though we do not share the same parents.

For example, Turkey dispatched over ten rescue team members to Taiwan, even though they had their own calamity to take care of. When Turkey was devastated by the earthquake there, a local Taiwanese businessman, Hu Kuang-chung, asked if Taiwan had dispatched rescue teams to that country. In fact, Tzu Chi members from Taiwan were already there to extend our helping hands.

I was told that the Hong Kong media had asked why China offered US$100,000 worth of relief supplies to help Taiwan.

They obtained the following answer: It was because when China had its disasters, Tzu Chi members from Taiwan were there to help. This human character of mutual love is truly beautiful. Only unconditional Great Love can erase hatred. The ugliest things in life are selfish love and hatred; the most beautiful are Great Love and tender-heartedness. This disaster revealed true love that does not discriminate against race, skin color, or religion. Everyone's common goal is to offer love.

At disaster scenes here in Taiwan, it was very touching to see foreign rescue workers risking their lives to search for survivors. I also hoped that during this disaster, the Taiwanese people would reach a common agreement—to stand united in carrying out this rescue mission.

The follow-up work after the earthquake was a little disorganized. There were too many supplies—they were stacked high and in no proper order. They were exposed to the sun, and one wondered if some supplies would rot or if the survivors really even needed them. There was no answer to these questions. When the goods were delivered, they were simply piled on top of each other; and with so many vehicles delivering supplies, traffic was just a mess.

There were problems with the health of survivors in the disaster areas. For example, most houses in Puli were in ruins, and the health of the residents there became an issue. Therefore, I told our commissioners that we should gather our resources and build temporary washrooms for the people there. There were also many people without homes—their damaged houses had fallen, cracked or tilted, and no one dared to stay inside. Hence, our mission was to quickly build some prefabricated houses for these people to settle in.

There was also the issue of victims' corpses. The bodies that were dug up were often mutilated or decomposed beyond description. They had to be appropriately handled and covered with cloth to prevent the stench from escaping. In addition, there was a need to quickly help family members with burial or cremation arrangements.

Those who were lucky enough to come through the disaster without injury also needed help. Tzu Chi members went to Puli, a town of over 100,000, to provide hot food and comfort to frightened and shocked residents twenty-four hours a day. I am grateful to all Tzu Chi members and the loving general public who gave their best to helping residents in the disaster areas.

Taiwanese immigrants in America were very concerned about relatives in Taiwan. They hoped to obtain news about their relatives through Tzu Chi offices in the States. Many of them also donated money and helped raise funds. At the Tzu Chi branch office in Southern California, crew members from nine local TV stations provided extended live coverage of the events there. They would film every time someone stepped in to donate money or called to express their concern.

The phone lines at the Tzu Chi offices were kept very busy. People from the commercial world were keen to coordinate their fund-raising activities in America. Medical doctors in America were also anxious to return to Taiwan to help. This love emanating from all corners of the world was very touching.

This disaster of the century has been a big shock to Taiwan. May all who have gone through this disaster learn to keep showing concern to others and bear in mind the conviction that Great Love transcends all boundaries. When we constantly show our care and concern to others, they will do the same to us when we need help. We need to have this mutual concern for other people. That is what I mean when I say, "When others are hurt, I feel the pain; when others suffer, I feel the sorrow."

The Power of Goodness

An entrepreneur who owned a big enterprise flew to eastern Taiwan to see me. With tears in his eyes, he said, "I feel ashamed of my uncaring behavior. In the past, you tried very hard to promote international relief work. The fund-raising for Turkey's earthquake victims, your words, and the diligent fund-raising efforts by Tzu Chi people did motivate me a little. But I soon forgot about it, because I felt Turkey was so far away and what happened over there had nothing to do with me. Now that an earthquake has struck Taiwan, I can sense the pain and feel deeply connected to it."

In the past few months, I have continuously urged everyone to put love into action. I have two intentions. First, I want people to be mindful and ready for crises or unexpected events in times of peace. Natural disasters are frightening. Taiwan is not big. When a natural disaster strikes, the outcome can be unimaginably tragic. Second, I want to remind people that man-made calamities can be very cruel. Everyone needs to be aware of the importance of Great Love—altruism.

I told this entrepreneur that the proportion of Taiwanese who practice charity on a long-term basis is not impressive. He said, "Master, although I am your disciple, I cannot be considered a loyal member of Tzu Chi because I have not regularly donated money."

He had many businesses and had been very generous in making contributions for the quake victims in Taiwan. So I told him, "It's not too late—from now on you can influence many people to do good deeds." For instance, he could begin with his business and encourage his employees to regularly donate money or offer their services to the needy. I told him what I needed the most were new members, but their donations did not need to be large. If they sincerely donated just a small amount of money every month, every penny of it would help create a thought of helping others. This thought would cultivate blessings. What was most needed was for more people to unite their thoughts of helping others, and to do so regularly and persistently.

I told him that after we had finished all the relief programs, we needed to promote the idea of constantly doing good deeds. The fact is that only permanent members of Tzu Chi can strengthen the power of kindness. Otherwise, the forces of greed, anger and delusion will wipe out people's intentions to do good. Only by summoning the forces of goodness can we maintain good and evil in balance. When we can activate the forces of goodness a bit more strongly in our society, it will become the bodhisattvas' Pure Land.

I am very grateful to overseas Tzu Chi members who have come forward to raise funds. Both Chinese residents and local natives in countries abroad have warmly responded to these fund-raising activities. They have remitted the donations back to Taiwan and continued to raise money. There are many moving stories in Taiwan as well. For instance, an eighty-year-old grandfather whose hands were amputated after a car accident donated NT$50,000 [US$1,600] at a Tzu Chi donation booth. It was all money that he had painstakingly earned by selling gum and candy. Two Mormons rode their bicycles by a construction site where many Tzu Chi volunteers were hard at work building houses for quake victims. Feeling that they should also do something for the victims, they got thirty other foreigners to come help. These young Americans said that they felt blessed, and they wanted to share their blessings with others. They were therefore willing to toil under the scorching sun and accept any job assigned to them. Life without love is swathed in darkness. Only love equally and selflessly given can transcend political, racial, cultural and religious boundaries.

All this has given me much confidence and hope. To accompany earthquake victims and their families along this long and arduous path, we need the care of Tzu Chi members from all over the world. Hence, we should resolve to be people who can help others and to do so promptly. It is rather sad when we find ourselves in a situation where we need help from others.

Someone asked me whether it was because we did not do good deeds, or we did not do enough of them, that we had to suffer this devastating disaster in September 1999. I have said before that there are over 22 million people living in Taiwan, but the proportion of Tzu Chi members who offer their love on a recurrent basis is only one in twenty. Is this good enough? It is like a baseball game. If there are a few good pitchers or catchers on a team but there is no team spirit or sense of camaraderie, will the team win the game? Similarly, the Buddha has told us about the concept of common karma. [The karma or destinies of a group of people are usually inter-related. For instance, when some people in a community pay no attention to environmental protection and keep cutting down trees, other people living in the same community might suffer due to mudslides or an environment vulnerable to hurricanes.] We will be blessed and will cultivate good fortune and a force of kindness when a majority of people in our society are kind and are willing to do good deeds.

Even after this disaster, we must still be grateful. Think about this: an earthquake of over 7.3 on the Richter scale rocked the whole of Taiwan, yet the majority of the people were safe. This is fortunate indeed. When our evil thoughts accumulate, calamities fall upon us. When all our good thoughts converge, then calamities can be dissolved and blessings will be bestowed upon us. Compared to the disaster areas of Chichi and Puli in central Taiwan, the areas that were relatively unaffected by the earthquake can be said to have encountered a strong karmic retribution but got away with little harm. Of course, our hearts ache when we look at those areas devastated by the earthquake. However, Tzu Chi members will accompany the residents in these places down this painful, arduous path.

Free from Delusion at the End

Savor the finale of life through simple yet touching stories.
Minds attaining peace and freedom exclaim sounds of joy.
The path from life to death carries the annotation of Truth.

A Lovely Lady

Two elderly ladies once underwent open-heart surgeries at the Tzu Chi General Hospital in Hualien. One of them—ninety years old—was the oldest person in southeast Asia to have a heart operation.

The elderly lady was diagnosed as having a coronary occlusion. After much deliberation, our doctors decided to perform surgery on her for three reasons. First, she was optimistic, understanding and loving towards her sons and daughters-in-law. Second, her children had always treated her with filial respect and had been looking after her. Third, the doctors were confident that the medical team and volunteers in the hospital would take good care of the lady.

The day after the operation, a volunteer visited the old lady, who was awake and in good spirits. She eagerly asked the volunteer, "When can I be discharged?" "Why are you in such a hurry to go home?" asked the volunteer. "I miss working in my vegetable garden." Evidently the old lady was used to doing physical work in her everyday life, which must have been one of the factors that led to her speedy recovery.

After the volunteer told me about this lady, I went to see her in the hospital. Her three sons, three daughters-in-law and a daughter were gathered by her bedside. "Wow, what a big, happy family you have!" I said as I stepped into the room.

I went up to her bedside and said to her, "You are very lucky indeed. Are you happy?"

"Yes, I'm very happy," she replied.

"You don't look at all like a patient who has just undergone an operation."

"That's because your doctors here are really good."

"And you are a brave patient." My comment brought a cheerful smile to her face.

"When are you going back to work in your vegetable garden?" I asked her.

"How did you know about that?"

"I've heard that you're eager to go home so that you can work in your garden again. What kinds of vegetables do you plant?" She rattled off a few kinds of vegetables.

"What do you plant during this season?" I asked her.

"Loofah gourds."

"Are you sure? Aren't loofahs harvested in summer? It's winter now."

"Yes, they're harvested in summer. But you have to start planting them now so that the vines have enough time to grow."

"How many children do you have?"

"Eight."

"Eight children including your daughters?"

"No, I have eight sons."

"Don't you have any daughters?"

"Yes, I have three."

I smiled. "Aren't you being a little biased? I asked you how many children you have and you only mentioned your sons."

"Only my sons are really my children. Sons bring daughters-in-law into the family while daughters are married off."

Her daughter standing by her bedside playfully protested, "You are being unfair, Mom!" All of us burst into laughter.

"You gave birth to your daughters as well," I said to the old lady. "So how many children do you have altogether?"

"Eleven of them." What a lovely lady she was.

The other patient was eighty-six years old. Both of them had had successful heart operations. If we hadn't built this hospital, these old folks and other emergency patients would have had little chance of survival in Hualien County, an area which had few medical facilities before. The mission of medicine is in fact important to the functioning of life. What is the most valuable thing in life? It is life itself! If we lose our lives, what would there be left to make our lives valuable?

Tzu Chi built its hospital out of respect for life. All our four missions of charity, medical service, educational development and cultural promotion are in fact the realization of this conviction. They might be arduous missions, but we will devote ourselves and spare no efforts to uphold our convictions.

The Little Bodhisattva

People with fortitude and perseverance are likely to succeed in all their undertakings. Similarly, patients with strong fortitude and perseverance eventually overcome their illnesses and regain the vigor of life.

During our winter relief distribution one year, the Tzu Chi office in Tachia invited all its aid recipients to a New Year's Eve dinner. In the middle of the feast, someone suddenly shouted, "His arm is bleeding!" Everyone turned and saw a little boy who had on his arm a huge tumor thicker than his thigh. It had split open, and blood and pus were flowing from the wound. The scene was horrible. Everyone panicked, not knowing what to do.

The boy said calmly with a smile, "Don't worry, just give me some toilet paper. That'll do it." Someone quickly went off and brought back a pile of toilet paper. The boy took some and pressed it against his wound. The courage of this little boy, who looked barely ten years old, touched everyone there.

After the incident, a Tzu Chi commissioner brought the boy to the Tzu Chi Hospital for treatment. I met him every time I paid a visit to the hospital. He was a very lovely boy, always smiling. I asked him once, "Does your arm still hurt?" He replied, with his usual smile, "No, but even if it does, I'll just let it be."

One day, one of our volunteers in the hospital told me that the tumor was malignant and the boy's arm had to be amputated. I went to his ward and asked him, "What has the doctor told you?" He said calmly, "The doctor said my arm must be amputated." I asked, "So what is your decision?" He just smiled but did not give me a reply. I said, "That arm is a sick arm. It's no longer yours. Be brave and have it amputated, okay?" He still smiled silently.

I asked him again, "After the amputation, you must live a meaningful life. Do you want to make a vow?" A volunteer standing to the side tried to encourage him, "Come on, make a vow. What do you want to do after you recover?" He then made his vow: "If I recover, I will become a Tzu Chi member."

I teased him, saying, "You aren't very ambitious, are you? You only want to be a Tzu Chi member, nothing more?" Another volunteer suggested to him, "You could vow to become a commissioner." He plucked up his courage and said, "Yes, if I recover, I want to become a Tzu Chi commissioner and volunteer." I said, "That's settled then—in the future you'll become a Tzu Chi commissioner and volunteer for life!"

After the amputation, the boy still wore his usual smile while he shuttled from one ward to another. During that time, he inspired many other patients in the hospital. There were some young motorcyclists who had injured themselves because of reckless riding. Their rehabilitation process was very painful, so he often went to cheer them up.

Later, when he was discharged from the hospital, he had to go to another hospital for chemotherapy. He always went alone because there was no one in his family who could go with him. His father was ill and his grandmother too old.

Although he is now only in ninth grade, he will soon begin training to become a commissioner. Once when I was in Tai-chung, a commissioner there showed me the boy's donor roster. He had already established forty regular donors. He said to the commissioner when he handed his roster to her, "After you have shown this to the Master, please give it back to me as soon as possible—I need it to raise more funds." His donors included his teachers, classmates, doctors and nurses. He really had the spirit of a commissioner.

Although his health was unstable, he never stayed in bed. On the contrary, he was always running around, meeting people and facing life courageously. This shows his fortitude and perseverance. Several times he was on the verge of death, but he faced the situation optimistically, never forgetting to wear his usual smile. Because of his positive attitude, he was always able to head off crises and to survive. He felt no hatred in his heart and did very well in school despite his illness. His willpower and resilience certainly command our respect.

The story of this little bodhisattva teaches us a lesson: a privileged childhood environment might be envied and desired by many people, but it is often an arduous environment which brings out the fortitude and perseverance in one's life.

An Accidental Gain

A newly married couple had a car accident in which the bridegroom was seriously injured. His leg was smashed, and he would have to wear an artificial limb for the rest of his life.

One day, I visited him in the hospital. The doctor was applying medicine to his wound. I asked him, "Does that hurt?"

He tried to hide his pain with a smile. "Master, you've said that if we turn the feeling of pain into a brisk sensation, it'll be over in no time. But if we see our pain as suffering, then it'll become difficult to endure. I've gained a certain insight into life through this accident—no one can predict what is going to happen, and misfortunes can occur in a split second."

"This is what we call the impermanence of life," I said. "But as long as your heart is not handicapped, you can share your experience with other patients when you recover. In this way, you'll actually teach Buddhism with yourself as an example and your encouragement will be more effective than my preaching. To patients suffering in pain, my consolation may sound casual and irresponsible since I haven't experienced their pain. On the other hand, you've been through such pain, faced it bravely and now live happily. You are an example to them. I'm sure they will be moved."

There are three states of sensation we experience throughout our lives—pain, pleasure, and neutrality. Our hearts usually feel according to what's going on around us. During meditation, those who can calm themselves down feel tranquil and at ease, whereas those who have never meditated before might find their bodies aching all over. Think about it:

is our perception of the conditions in our surroundings the result of our minds?

I often encourage patients to face their lot in life bravely and make the best use of their lives. I ask them not to indulge their minds in pain, but instead to turn the feeling of pain or suffering into productive energy. I also tell them, "You're fortunate that your injury is not fatal. When you have recuperated, you'll be able to walk out of this ward with a healthy body and make the best use of your abilities. If you think like this, you'll feel relaxed and happy."

I once visited a patient who was injured at work. When a volunteer told him, "The Master is here to see you," he was very happy and sat up in bed at once. I asked him, "How did you injure yourself?" He said, "I work at the military airfield in Hualien, where I was accidentally hit by a brass chain. I'm very grateful to you, Master. You built such a good hospital and the doctors here are excellent. I've been here two weeks already and I don't think that this is suffering. I feel no pain at all!"

"I think my wife and daughter are indeed fortunate that I'm only slightly injured," he continued. "If that heavy chain had hit my head, the consequences would have been unthinkable. Maybe it's because I've done some good deeds that I was able to escape a catastrophe. The volunteers here have been very kind. I'm really touched by them! I'll make a vow to be a vegetarian from now on." [Most of the volunteers at the Tzu Chi hospitals are vegetarians who are compassionate enough to avoid eating meat]

"May you be blessed," I said. "This is a turning point in your life. It will be even better if you also stop smoking and drinking." He said, "I stopped smoking and drinking long ago. However, I used to have many love affairs. Now that I've vowed to become a vegetarian, I'll change that too."

This is what we call "a blessing brought about from misfortune." Although the man had been injured, he gained a kind, complete heart. That is why I have always said that a physical handicap is not the worst thing that can happen to a person. Rather it is a mental handicap which often brings tribulation to oneself, one's family and society.

There was another patient who had been knifed by a friend. "After this incident, I learned a lot about life," the patient said to me. He was stabbed by a friend who had had lost all his money in gambling and asked to borrow some from him. When he turned his friend down, the friend became furious and tried to kill him. He said that the Tzu Chi Hospital had indeed saved his life and he was very grateful to Tzu Chi.

I said to him, "You must let bygones be bygones and not allow your mind to cling to the incident."

"I will forgive him, Master," he said. "In fact after I was brought to this hospital, I realized that there are many people out there who really care about me."

"If that is so, then all is not lost," I told him. "If one can be considerate to others and learn to forgive and forget, one will accumulate blessings for oneself. To have an accommodating heart is a blessing indeed."

I mentioned the newlyweds who had an auto accident. Both the husband and wife were seriously injured. The driver of the car that collided with theirs was also injured, but not as badly. I bumped into him in the corridor when he was about to be discharged, and I said to him, "Come back to visit that young couple when you have time. As humans, we all have feelings for each other. Besides, they were badly hurt."

"I will certainly come back to visit them often," he said, "As it turned out, after the accident we found out that we actually come from the same town. We are all from Chiayi."

The power of karma in our lives is mysterious and unfathomable. Therefore, we must seize every moment by reminding ourselves not to create bad karma with our bodies and not to have evil thoughts in our minds. Our minds have control over our actions. A thought arises in the mind and leads to a subsequent action, which always produces karma.

The power of karma exists in two forms: in the first form we are influenced by the karma we have created in our past lives, and in the second we meet other people in our present lives by the karmic causes in this life. Together, they produce the vicissitudes of life and the happy or regrettable relationships between people, all of which happens within a blink of the eye. Hence, we should always be alert and mindful of our thoughts and actions in our everyday life.

A Real Superwoman

In life we have to face many adversities and our wishes do not always come true. Nevertheless, we need not feel completely helpless because with fortitude and confidence we are able to pull through the difficulties in life.

I once met a woman who was born with abnormal joints in both legs. Because her parents could not afford medical treatments for her, she grew up crippled and often had to endure the aches in her joints. Later she married a man who was also from a poor family. They remained financially strapped. Fortunately, with her fortitude she endured the hardships without complaining. However, excessive labor soon tired her out and her joints deteriorated so badly that she could barely stand.

Her family took her to the Hualien Tzu Chi Hospital. The condition was diagnosed as very rare and complicated. The head of the osteopathy department employed an advanced technique to operate on her joints. The operation proved to be very successful and the technique became an international medical breakthrough.

When I visited her in the hospital, she looked cheerful and wore a bright smile on her face. She had just gone through an operation that lasted more than ten hours and her legs were still suspended in the air, but that didn't seem to affect her. She even cracked jokes with her visitors. Her positive attitude made her a very good patient.

Her doctor told me that he had never treated that condition before. The treatment she was undergoing was in fact experimental. However, he had confidence in her. He was right. She made rapid progress, and at last she could stand up properly. I was truly happy for her. The torment that she had endured her whole life was finally coming to an end. During her three or four months in the hospital, she made friends with the doctors, nurses and other patients there. When she was finally discharged, she left happily.

Time passed, and then during one of my rounds in the hospital I heard that she had tried to commit suicide and was in the emergency ward. After she was revived and transferred to a regular ward, I went over to see her. When she saw me, she grabbed my hand, called out "Master," and then burst into tears. I patted her shoulder and teased her: "How silly of you! Why have you done such a foolish thing to yourself? So many people here spent so much time and effort in taking care of you. If we had known that you would try to commit suicide, then we wouldn't have bothered treating you at all! Why did you try to kill yourself?"

She said she could not stand her mother-in-law's tongue-lashings. "Your mother-in-law reproaches you because she cares about you," I told her. "You're being unkind to her if you kill yourself over this. You've already spent so much time and effort in getting your legs to function properly. Are you going to let all the pain that you've been through simply go to waste? Each day of your life has a value of its own. You should live well and make the best use of your life."

A few days later, I visited her again. "Do you still wish to end your life?" I asked her. "No, I'll live happily from now on," she said with a smile. "I'm going to live a happy life and be confident and brave."

At Chinese New Year, she came to visit me and show me that she had been living well. She said, "Master, I can walk steadily and gracefully now. I was on cloud nine when I was able to walk to the post office and back without the help of a cane!" She looked very happy indeed.

This is a remarkable woman with a strong will. What she encountered in life would have easily defeated many others. Although she still had little money, her positive attitude made each day full of happiness. There are many challenges and hardships in life, but a hardworking person with an optimistic attitude will conquer them all.

Luck Grows out of Adversity

It is a law of nature that the sky always clears up after a storm. But in the case of the human body, things might not return to normal again after an accident.

On Labor Day, a train driver was admitted to Tzu Chi hospital. It was his day off, and the day had begun with joy when he took his little girl out to play. Her hands were dirty, so he took her to the gutter by the roadside to rinse off her hands. Just as he was bending down, a car driving at high speed hit them from behind. The girl was thrown by the great impact, while his pelvis was smashed. It was later discovered that the reckless driver had just killed two other people and was speeding away in panic.

The train driver could not accept the fact that he had become handicapped. It was indeed hard for someone who used to be full of vigor to accept such cruelty. Yet this type of accident is not rare in life. Misfortune can happen in a split second.

And how could the car driver have expected that he would cause two deaths and two casualties? Because of him, the deceased were gone forever and the injured would have to live the rest of their lives in pain. Though he himself was not hurt physically, the enormous mental agony that he will have to endure is no less tormenting.

The human body is a small, fragile universe. We might be healthy and sound today, but there is no guarantee that we will remain the same for the rest of our years. The man had worked as a train driver for many years, transporting any number of passengers to their destinations every day. Yet a car accident took away his abilities in just a blink of an eye. He might have taken his abilities and health for granted. But now, no matter how hard he might try, he would never again use his legs to walk freely. This is what the Buddha called "impermanence."

Nature, or the great universe, has the ability to recover. After a heavy storm, the sky will surely clear up. If the wind knocks a tree down, it will live on if we stand it up again. If a flood ravages a field, it will be ready for farming the next year. However, the little universe of the human body is not as resilient, and it only has a life span of several decades. Although our wisdom life is everlasting, yet without this body we will have to wait for an unpredictable rebirth.

The wisdom life is always with us as we go through the cycle of reincarnation. It is our life "energy," which carries on life after life. When this life ends, the wisdom life accompanies us to the next one. Therefore, we must diligently cultivate it.

The train driver had become physically disabled and his body would never be "normal" again. However, if through this incident he is able to realize the truth of life, he can still make himself useful. He can use his mouth and hands to do good deeds, and with his real-life experience he can encourage other patients who have been struck with a similar misfortune. In this way, he can accumulate merits and cultivate his wisdom life.

If he had not been struck with such misfortune, he might never have pondered the meaning of life. He would probably just have carried on his routine of eating, resting and working. But the unexpected accident provided him with a chance to meet many loving Tzu Chi volunteers in our hospital and he gained a deeper understanding of life. It was a good chance for him to cultivate his wisdom life. In this way, even though he must adjust to his physical disability, he will still be able to live a beautiful life.

Life in the Hospital

In the hospital, we meet people from all walks of life and everyone has his or her own life story. The more we see, the more we realize that we must not waste our lives and time.

There was an old woman undergoing rehabilitation therapy. The therapist placed a mirror in front of her and encouraged her to lift her head and look into the mirror, but she was too weak. Dejection and helplessness were written all over her face.

I asked the therapist where her family members were. The therapist said, "They never visit her." The poor old woman! How I wished I could hold her by her arms and help her walk forward. But both her legs were disabled, so how could I make her walk even one step?

The old woman must have had a very hard time taking care of her family when she was younger. Yet in her old age she had no one by her side to take care of her. Worse still, she was ill and could hardly move. It was only natural that her heart was filled with grief and indignation. The expression on her face was simply heartbreaking.

The rehabilitation process is usually long and tedious. While some patients are very pessimistic, others are strong-willed. Among the patients in rehabilitation, there was a handsome young man who had been very enthusiastic in recovering the use of his body and learning to move his legs again.

I heard that he was an electrician who had been injured at work. He was installing electrical equipment at a construction site when a casting mold fell on him and injured his spinal cord. The chance of complete recovery was very slim. Nevertheless, he had high expectations and full confidence in himself.

I often saw him at one corner of the rehabilitation room, where there was a pair of handrails. With his hands on the handrails for support, he made great efforts to swing his lower body forward. He sweated profusely during the exercise, yet the bright smile on his face never faded.

He said he considered himself fortunate, for he could still use his hands to support his body while other patients in the rehabilitation room had lost the use of all four of their limbs. Looking at him trying so hard with his exercises, I was really moved.

"Take a break," I urged him.

"I can still carry on for one more round," he said as he swung himself from end to end. First his hands began to tremble, then his whole body was trembling, but still he was smiling. He had no complaints whatsoever, but he demonstrated an enormous willpower and courage that touched everyone.

In the infants' intensive care unit, premature babies are placed in incubators. Their little bodies, which are only the size of an adult's palm, are dark red and stuck all over with little tubes. Their lives, as flimsy as those tiny tubes inserted in them, could snap very easily. The parents of these babies must suffer great anxiety and agony.

In the obstetrics ward I met a young pregnant woman who was trying to walk to the birthing room. She was holding her stomach and her expression revealed that she was in great pain. Her husband and her mother-in-law helped her forward, but she could hardly move a step. "This is a moment to remember," I encouraged her. "You are going to give birth to your baby. Now try to relax!" She tried to put on a smile, but the pain seemed excruciating. This is the prelude to the birth of a new life. A mother has to suffer great pain before the child is born. When the child finally comes safely into the world, no one can predict what his or her future will be.

There was a chubby six-month-old baby in the infants' intensive care unit. Her face was like the full moon, fair and lovely, but she had become a vegetable. A high fever in her third month had damaged her brain. The baby girl had a wonderful mother who had resigned from her teaching position in order to give her baby girl complete care.

Life has many different facets indeed. Therefore, when we are blessed with a healthy, able body, we should make the best use of our abilities and not waste our lives away.

The Source of Life and Wisdom

We all face life differently. A physically healthy person may be filled with anguish and distress or have a morbid state of mind. This is called "illness of the mind." On the other hand, a happy, optimistic person might be in poor health. There are illnesses of the body and also those of the mind, and together they form the imperfections of life.

I heard of a female patient who had a very healthy mind. Her physical condition was so complicated that the doctors could find no treatment for her. However, when she talked about her illness, she took it as lightly as if she were talking about somebody else's.

She was only in her thirties, yet she had been afflicted with a rare disease for more than ten years. Many times she had come close to crossing the threshold between life and death, but she was able to remain calm during each crisis because she had prepared herself mentally.

Recently, she was hospitalized again because of a high blood sugar level. When I visited her, she told me about her condition casually as if it were not her business. "Two or three days ago, the doctors tried a new drug on me," she told me. "They gave me a shot and told the nurse to keep me awake, as my body might have a bad reaction to the medicine. If I had fallen asleep, I might never have woken up again."

The patient herself was a nurse by profession. Her doctor encouraged her: "You should make a vow to volunteer your services when you recover. You could come with me to remote mountainous regions and serve the aborigines. But first of all you have to learn their language so that you can communicate with them." As she was going through a critical time with the new drug, she exercised all her willpower to stay awake. Most of the time she talked to an old aboriginal woman who shared the ward with her. The old woman had been moaning and groaning with pain. In order to help the old woman forget the pain, the younger patient sang songs with her. She also asked the old woman to teach her the aboriginal language. The old woman had been feeling very lonely in the hospital, which made the pain even more difficult to bear. When the patient talked with the old woman, the old woman was able to forget her pain and the patient was able to learn some simple aboriginal phrases.

The patient's extremely high blood sugar level had caused the blood vessels in her eyeballs to rupture. Her vision was seriously impaired and she would see double. What touched me deeply was that she did not stop writing, even under such difficult conditions. I asked her, "How are your eyes today?" She said, "I started to write about two or three days ago." She took out a draft from the bedside drawer and showed it to me. "I see double when I look at the words, but I keep working at it." With clear, neat handwriting, she had written an inspiring account of all she had been through during her illness..

In the previous two or three days her blood glucose level had remained high, especially after she took her medicine. What was worse, her mouth blistered after her doctor tried another drug on her. When the blisters burst, it was extremely painful. The doctor let her suck a kind of painkiller meant for cancer patients so that she could talk. She was still sucking on the pill when she talked to me, but didn't seem to be bothered by the pain at all.

Every time she came close to death, she exercised her willpower and survived. She was a good example of a patient with a truly healthy state of mind. We can see that no matter how quickly medical science progresses, the most effective treatment still lies within oneself. Illness is the result of physical factors and one's state of mind. I have seen patients who are thirty percent ill physically, but seventy percent ill mentally. Such people always think that they have fallen gravely ill. By thinking so, they are in fact making themselves both physically and psychologically ill.

To live a healthy life requires a healthy state of mind, which in turn will provide us with a happy life. The purpose of learning Buddhism is to learn the ways to a healthy life, while a tenacious willpower is our source of life and wisdom.

Sick Body, Healthy Mind

In the hospital, we see people living in adversity and illness. To become ill is indeed distressing! That's why we should make full use of our lives when we are healthy. To possess a healthy body is the greatest luxury of life.

One time when I was visiting the hospital, a volunteer came up to me and said, "Master, can you please come and look at a patient? He really wants to see you."

"What's wrong with him? What's his condition now?" I asked.

"He has uremia. He's very depressed and refuses to cooperate with the doctor."

"Alright, I'll be there in a moment."

Then I remembered that a Tzu Cheng Faith Corps volunteer who helped out at the Abode of Still Thoughts had been sent to the hospital a few days before because of a sudden gastric hemorrhage. I decided to visit him first, and asked the nurse to show me the way. The nurse told me, "This volunteer has helped us out a lot here."

"How can he be of help when he is ill?"

"Yesterday we got a patient with alcohol poisoning. He was brawling and making a big fuss. We were lucky to have that volunteer here. He tried to calm the patient down and counsel him. He saved us a lot of trouble."

When I walked into the ward, I saw the volunteer sitting by another patient who occupied the bed across from his. He was speaking softly to the patient. I asked him, "How is he doing?" He replied, "He just has a bad case of the flu." I knew that he said this so that the patient wouldn't be embarrassed.

It was no wonder that the patient readily obeyed his words. Although the volunteer was ill, he did not give up his usual role in the hospital. He was indeed a role model of someone who was physically ill but mentally healthy.

"I'm sorry to let you worry about me, Master," the volunteer said. "It's an old ailment of mine. I'm having a relapse. Our hospital is really great. After being here for a day and a night, I'm much better. What I need now is rehabilitation. I can be discharged today." Even though he was ill and hospitalized, he did not fail to seize every chance to help others. This is what I call making the best use of one's life. I was both touched by him and happy for him.

As I walked out of the ward, another nurse came up to me. "Will you come to see one more patient, Master?"

"What is the problem?"

"She is in the final stage of cancer. She had a nightmare last night and felt depressed when she woke up. Can you please take a look at her?"

So I went to the cancer patients' ward. A doctor was talking to her and trying to cheer her up. She looked nervous. I said to her, "It's natural to fall ill, but when the body is ill the mind should not fall ill as well. A day will pass by whether you are happy or sad, so why not live it happily? You should leave the illness of your body to the doctor and the illness of your mind to the Buddha. You must have faith!" She looked calmer and said to me with a smile, "Yes, Master, I'll chant 'Amitabha' more often."

It must have been difficult for her to stay calm when she was in the final stage of cancer. Most people are afraid of death. What can we do when we are confronted with it? We must first have peace of mind, but that is not easily attained. In life, many things are beyond our control. We have this body, yet we have no control over it when we are ill. It is easy to tell others, "Take it easy, let it go!" But what if we are in the same situation?

Later, I went to see the uremia patient as I had promised. The patient, who also had asthma and diabetes, coughed incessantly. He moaned, "I don't really like sweet food, so why have I become diabetic?"

I tried to console him. "Diabetes is not exclusively a disease for people with a sweet tooth. You have to be conscious of your daily lifestyle and eating habits. You look great today! Don't worry, you'll be fine."

Life is unpredictable. We should make the best use of our life when we are healthy, or else we will regret it. Illness is not exclusive to old people. Whether we are in adolescence, middle age or old age, we should seize every moment and live every day to the fullest.

The key chapter in the *Great Conduct Bodhisattva Sutra* states, "When a day has passed, your life span is diminished, like fish swimming in draining water. What happiness is there in such a life? You should zealously progress in goodness and eliminate evil with the same urgency as if your hair had caught on fire. Be aware of the impermanence of the world and be not idle."

A Fallen Angel

On the third floor of the Hualien Tzu Chi Hospital building are the wards for obstetrics and pediatrics patients. One day when I was walking past the wards, I heard a nurse call out the name "Nan-nan." This was a familiar name to me, so I asked, "Is Nan-nan here again?" I walked into the ward to see him.

Nan-nan was a little boy suffering from atrophy who had been in and out of the hospital many times. Almost every time he was hospitalized, he had to stay several months. This was a little boy devastated by his illness. The virus had now spread to his brain, resulting in recurring spasms. He was wearing an oxygen mask when I saw him. When I stroked his head, I found that he was soaked through with cold sweat. Poor boy!

I walked into another wing and the nurse there told me, "Wei-wei is here." This was another familiar name to me. Wei-wei was a one-year-old boy who had just been learning to walk. When his mother wasn't looking, he walked out of the house and onto the road. A car came and ran over him. When he arrived at the hospital he had already stopped breathing, but the staff brought him back to life again. He was later transferred to the intensive care unit. When I visited him at the beginning of the month, I saw that this chubby, lovely child had turned into a vegetable who could make no sound even when he cried as he had undergone a tracheotomy. I couldn't help but grieve for him.

There and then, the doctor explained his condition to me. "His chances of recovering are very slim. He can't breathe on his own, and because his spine was injured he can't move at all." I held his left hand and felt some response, but the doctor said it was limited to that small area.

I asked, "Can he feel anything?"

The doctor replied, "He doesn't seem to have any consciousness."

"Is there no other way to save him?"

"His spine and ligaments were all crushed. Even if a miracle happens, the nerves and ligaments will take at least a thousand days to grow back to normal."

One thousand days—that is more than three years! The poor child would have to lie in bed for three years, and still no one could say whether after that long wait he would regain consciousness, move freely, or breathe on his own again.

After some time, I visited Wei-wei again. Both mother and child were sound asleep when I entered the room. I stroked Wei-wei's face. He woke up and cried in a very weak voice. The nurse told me, "He can call 'Mama' now. When we cover the opening in his trachea, he can make the sound 'Mama.'" Not only that, he was also able to move his hands and legs energetically. It had been only eighteen days since I last saw him. His speedy recovery was record-breaking. When his mother held him in her arms, he would kick briskly. He looked really adorable. Life is full of miracles, just like the one which happened to Wei-wei.

Life is precious. Yet many of us might think after seeing him suffer that it would be better for Nan-nan to leave his life and be liberated. However, one cannot leave before one has fulfilled one's karma in this life. On the other hand, Wei-wei was blessed with a miraculous recovery one thousand days early.

The most blessed thing in life is a healthy body and the ability to move around freely. Little one-year-old Wei-wei met with a mishap just because of a careless action, but he had a tenacious life force. The doctor had already proclaimed him a young vegetable, yet his bodily functions eventually recovered. This was indeed unbelievable!

We can see that if people have not completed their karma, they cannot end their lives no matter how much they want to. On the other hand, when people have less bad karma and more blessings, even if they are on the verge of death, they will eventually be able to regain their health and the right to use their lives. We should seize the days when we are healthy, as life is impermanent. The only way to perpetuate our right to use our impermanent life is to contribute all that we can every minute and every second.

Return to the Original Nature

We have all experienced illness of the body. Some of us have experienced illness of the mind. Such people are often unhappy and discontent, and they always give their own interests top priority. Being suspicious and unwilling to love or be compassionate to others are also manifestations of an ill mind.

Some people are overly concerned with their own bodies and anxious about the slightest sign of trouble. A headache implies a brain tumor, and a stomachache makes them suspect that they have cancer. All physical problems are perceived with pessimism.

When people ask me why they often feel ill, I tell them that when they are ill they should consult a doctor. Surprisingly many have already been to a doctor. Although the doctor reassured them that they were healthy, they still felt sick. Indeed they were sick, yet the sickness was not in their bodies, but in their minds. If they had a thorough understanding of the body and mind, then they would be able to let go of all anxieties.

The Buddha once said, "All phenomena are illusions." Anything that has form is unreal, since it will change sooner or later. Being attached to one's physical and psychological states, which are both illusory, will only bring suffering. What is real then? The one real thing we should try to attain in our spiritual cultivation is a return to our original pure nature, which has been contaminated by the environment we live in and by the people we interact with.

Depending on the environment we live in, all of us pick up different customs and beliefs. For example, newborns will learn to speak whatever language is spoken to them. The diversity of our behaviors can be compared to a human face. Although everyone has a pair of eyes, a nose, a mouth, a pair of ears, and two eyebrows, we all look different. Even identical twins have unique features that enable their parents to differentiate them. Yet, despite our differences, we all have one thing in common—our original pure nature.

The *Trimetrical Classic* [a traditional Chinese children's primer] states, "In the beginning, all human nature is good." This good nature is the most thorough, pure and enduring buddha-nature. In contrast, our bodies are constantly changing and will one day cease to exist. These illusory bodies create many sufferings in this world, so we should not be attached to them. Once we have taken our last breath, this phase of our life ends. Our consciousness will leave this body to find its karmic destiny as it brings us to another phase of life.

In parts of Taiwan, some people still practice a certain custom: at the funeral of a parent, a married daughter should cry as she crawls back into the house and then vigorously shake the parent's dead body. People feel that this custom expresses the filial piety of the daughter. However to the deceased, such an expression of respect after death is no longer important. People should show their filial piety while their parents are alive. That is genuine filial piety. When one expels one's last breath, the crying and mourning of relatives will do no good. Instead, relatives should chant the holy name of "Amitabha" to comfort the soul of the dead and cultivate their own bodhi-mind [a determination to learn the Buddha's teachings and to redeem all living beings from their sufferings].

The most important goals in studying Buddhism are to get rid of bad habits, to return to one's original pure nature, to be good to others, and to broaden the mind to love, trust and forgive all souls under the heavens. In this way, we can gradually accomplish our altruistic missions.

Life is impermanent. We cannot avoid birth, aging, sickness and death. Every day our life becomes shorter. Therefore, don't let a day pass by in vain. We must seize every opportunity to learn.

A Mustard Seed

The key to a harmonious, happy, healthy life lies in extending respect and love to all creatures. Ordinary people love only those close to them. The Buddha taught us to broaden our minds to love all creatures in the world. But that is not easy, for to love only friends and relatives is a deeply rooted habit to which ordinary people tend to cling.

There is a story in a Buddhist sutra. A woman named Kilisha was born into a poor family. Her ancestors were originally rich, but had lost all their wealth. Kilisha was very beautiful. Her beauty fascinated a young man who came from a rich family. The young man asked his parents to let him marry her. When they were married, her impoverished parents could not afford to give her any dowry, so her in-laws and their servants looked down on her. [It was customary in India to marry one's daughter off to her husband's family with an abundant dowry; otherwise, she would run the risk of being despised. In fact, this custom can still be found in some regions in modern India]. Although she was the young mistress of the house, her position in the family was very low.

One day she became pregnant. She prayed to have a boy so that she could gain a higher standing in the family. Her wish was fulfilled and she indeed gave birth to a baby boy. As she had expected, she won the attention of the whole family and the respect of the servants, and she lived happily for a period of time.

However, the good times didn't last long. When the boy was one year old, he suddenly died from an acute illness.

Grief engulfed Kilisha. The mother held the dead boy in her arms and asked everyone she met to bring her baby back to life. One day she was told, "The Buddha is the only person in the world who can save your child." Immediately, she rushed to the abode where the Buddha was staying and fervently begged him to bring her son back to life. The Buddha said to her kindly, "There is a way to save your child, but first you have to calm down. Then I'll teach you how." The Buddha's words soothed her, and she listened to him attentively.

"You must go find a family that has never had a death," the Buddha instructed her. "Ask them to give you a mustard seed. This way your son will be saved."

"Obtaining a mustard seed shouldn't be too difficult," she thought. With high hopes, she visited one family after another. Although all the families had mustard seeds, there was not a single family that had never experienced death.

Kilisha was extremely disappointed. She went back to the Buddha and said to him, "Reverend Buddha, it is easy to get a mustard seed, but I could not find a family that has not had somebody die."

"Yes, as long as there is life, there is death," the Buddha said slowly. "Immortality cannot be wished for. There was only so much destined time between you and your son. Why ask for more?"

Hearing the Buddha's sincere words, Kilisha finally became peaceful. Now she understood that having unattainable wishes begets suffering in life and that there is karma which one must inevitably experience. She let go of her attachments to worldly life and beseeched the Buddha to allow her to become a nun. She became the most diligent of all in the assembly of nuns.

This story teaches us that we have no control over the length of our life. While it exists, cherish it. When we cannot keep it, let it go, for that is the natural course of life. For this reason, we must love each other and treasure our time together. We must love all living creatures in order to lead a happy human life.

A Free and Easy Life

Sickness not only causes physical pain, but it also triggers the fear that if it cannot be cured, death is imminent.

Death is a topic people avoid talking about. I remember that ten or twenty years ago when I started preaching, I stated, "The only thing one must learn in life is death; nothing else needs to be learned." At that time, some found my statement strange, for it contradicted the common belief that all things except death need to be learned.

Death must be learned. Most of us do not know why we were born into this world. This unawareness makes us live in confusion. To become aware, we have to talk about death. Then when our time comes to leave the world, we can do so happily and freely. That is what Buddhism means by being emancipated and at ease. If we can face death with this attitude, then we will understand clearly which realm we will enter in our next life. Thus we must probe both death and life and face death squarely. Avoiding it is unwise.

I once read the book *At Ease with Life and Death* by a Japanese professor. In this book, there is a fascinating true story.

There was an optimistic, humorous woman who was ninety-one years old and who had eleven children and lots of grandchildren. She had led a relatively good life. In her later years, she was afflicted with a terminal disease. Before she passed away, her sons invited a Catholic priest to say Mass for her.

Seeing that the old woman was still conscious, the priest said to her, "Now attend Mass with a devout heart." He sang hymns and prayed, and then suddenly the old lady sat up.

"Thank you for praying for me," she said to him. "Now I want all of you to do something for me." What did she want? "I want to drink some whiskey." When her children, who had been in the depths of grief, heard what she wanted, they immediately jumped up and poured a glass for her. She drank one mouthful and said, "It's too strong. Put some ice cubes in it to make it weaker and cooler." Her children did so.

After she finished the drink, she said, "That was good! Now light me a cigarette." Her son reminded her that the doctor had prohibited her from smoking and drinking. But she replied, "I'm the one who's dying, not the doctor." Her son could not refuse and lit a cigarette for her. She enjoyed smoking it.

After she finished smoking, she said to the priest, "Thank you for praying for me. I am going to Heaven now. Good-bye." With that, she closed her eyes and passed away peacefully. So it was that when her children were trapped in an abyss of grief, she woke up again and humorously talked to them. Their sadness was thus swept away.

After she was gone, everyone in the family said, "We should learn from her—she passed away so freely and serenely."

In Taiwan, a similar case was reported in the newspaper more than ten years ago. A seventy-year-old woman passed away. Her family members were preparing the funeral when she suddenly woke up and asked, "What are you doing?" They were all amazed and said, "Grandma, how come you woke up?"

The old woman said, "I haven't chewed my betel nut yet." Her children gave her a betel nut. After chewing it, she said with satisfaction, "Now I'm willing to die. I'm leaving you. Goodbye!" How free and easy her life was.

To sum up, with birth comes death—that is the natural course of life. With this understanding we can treat death with an optimistic attitude, not grief or anxiety. If we are peaceful and happy when our time to leave the world comes, then we will bring our families peace of mind.

Comprehend the Truth of Life

In this world everyone seems to be leading different lives, but in reality all work for and agonize over the human body. When the body comes in touch with its external circumstances, the mind starts to make distinctions and worries, and then it commands the body to act. If our actions are improper, then distress will eventually get the better of us. Therefore, we must guard our minds and behavior.

Because we think we own this body, we all worry about parting with it. Most of the time, the mere thought of getting sick and dying frightens us. However, people whose mindset has transcended that of ordinary people can be emancipated from such fear and anxiety, for they know that death is but a natural part of life.

There was a true story of a man who was sentenced to death because he had committed monstrous crimes. He was originally a troubled man, yet during his two short years of imprisonment he comprehended the truth of life and, incredibly, attained peace and was at ease with dying.

On the night of his execution, he dressed himself and prayed quietly like he always did. He calmly waited for the executioners to come and take him to the execution ground.

When he saw someone approaching, he immediately stood up ready to follow that man, but he was told, "Not you, somebody else." The second time he saw someone coming, he stood up again, calm and peaceful. However he was told again, "It's not you, it's somebody else."

If a doctor told us we were afflicted with a fatal disease, most of us would be tormented with worries and fear. However, this man faced his execution calmly, as if dying were as natural as going home.

When evil thoughts arise, suppress them right away. This way we can avoid disaster. When bad thoughts arise and we do not review and correct them, but instead follow the evil thoughts with action, then we create bad karma. This criminal did not understand Buddhism and spiritual cultivation until he read my lectures on *The Thirty-seven Principles of Enlightenment* in prison. After he read the book, he thoroughly repented of his sins and his troubled mind was emancipated. Therefore even on the day his life was to be taken, he could pray to the Buddha with ease and wait for the last moment with serenity.

His final wish was to return to Tzu Chi to do good deeds in his next life. When his wife took their children to see him, he reminded her repeatedly, "You must remember to take our children to visit Master Cheng Yen of the Tzu Chi Foundation. We are all her disciples." It is truly a pity that he had not had the chance to learn about Tzu Chi before he committed his crimes.

To study Buddhism is to train ourselves in our daily lives to accept calmly whatever we experience, even if it is disturbing. We must never be impetuous, behave inappropriately or create negative karma.

Our body is the source of most of our problems in life. Without the body, we would have fewer anxieties. In order to emancipate ourselves and regard death as natural as going home, we should use our spirituality as a shield against anything that comes our way and cultivate our minds in whatever circumstances we find ourselves.

Cause and Effect in Life and Death

Life is unpredictable. Who would have expected that a
fall from some scaffolding would take the life of a Tzu Chi
Honorary Board member from Changhua County? The man
was kindhearted and had a happy family. His wife was a
Tzu Chi commissioner engaged in doing good deeds. It was
hard to accept that a loving person like him should have
died in such a way. Inconceivable as it was, his sudden
death was a tragic fact.

His family, especially his mother, was heartbroken. Fortunately their belief in Buddhism gave them support, and
the care from Tzu Chi people greatly consoled them. When
I went to see his family, his mother asked me sadly, "My
son was a good person, obedient and dutiful. Why did he
leave us like this? I am so sad." As she recounted her son's
good points, I comforted her: "Your time with your son
was preconditioned in your previous life and it was impossible to change."

"But my son was a wonderful man. Why couldn't he have
escaped from this karma?" she asked. I told her that one's
karma cannot be altered. All one can do is to create good conditions and good relationships. The Buddha had a disciple
by the name of Maudgalyayana who was noted for his
supernatural powers. Even with his powers, he still could
not escape from the karma of being stoned to death by religious cultists. Some monks asked the Buddha why
Maudgalyayana couldn't defend himself when he had such
great powers. The Buddha answered, "Supernatural powers
cannot be used to fight against karma."

Karma is unchangeable. Even the Buddha himself fell ill sometimes. It was recorded that one day as the Buddha was walking, a small stick dug into his toe. The area became infected, and he developed a high fever and nearly lost consciousness.

Although life is impermanent and full of adversity, you can diminish suffering if you understand the nature of adversity. The Buddha said, "To know what you did in your previous life, look at what you are now; to predict what you will be in your next life, see what you are doing now." In this life, you reap what you sow. The effects of what you sowed in your past life you must bear happily, for they are your own doing.

Although karma is unalterable, relationships can be created. When you meet people that are difficult to get along with, try to accommodate and understand them and do not dispute with them. You can turn a bad karmic relationship into a good one. By doing this, you will not create more bad karma. You meet people with whom you do not see eye to eye in this life because you both planted seeds of mutual dislike in a previous life. In this life, the seed bore fruit, so you meet again. If you are still on bad terms, then the bad effect will again be manifest in your next life.

"Do not grieve any more," I said to the heartbroken mother. "Your time with your son was short because of karma. He had been a good son because you both cultivated good relationships before, and he could provide wealth for the family because he had abundant blessings. However, his destined time in this world was short, so he had an accident and was gone in an instant. Fortunately, he didn't suffer or leave his family in trouble. Besides, he had cultivated good conditions and good relationships. That is why so many brothers and sisters in the big Tzu Chi family came to offer you their blessings and care."

The man was carried home. His face had not been hurt in the fall. When members of the Tzu Cheng Faith Corps were changing his clothes, blood started flowing out of his ears and stained the clean clothes. It did not stop until after they had patiently changed four sets of clothing. Although he had no siblings, the brothers of the Tzu Cheng Faith Corps treated him better than blood relatives would have done.

His mother repeatedly expressed her gratitude to the Tzu Chi people who helped. "Because your son did good deeds and built good relationships, so many Tzu Chi people came to care and help," I told her. "His death taught us that although karma is unalterable, good relationships can be nurtured. If it weren't for the good relationships he built, no one would have come to extend their helping hands." With the care and support from the big Tzu Chi family, his family could stand on their own feet again.

Karma is unalterable but relationships can be created, so we have to be good to others to cultivate good relations. What we do in this life will affect our next life. This life is the result of everything we did in previous lives, so we have to accept cheerfully what this life brings. If we want to be joyful in the next life, we have to act with willingness and sincerity now. Please be mindful. Whatever comes to you is meant to be because of karma. Accept whatever may happen to you cheerfully, instead of complaining or rebelling against your fate. This way you will not create more bad karma and will be at ease.

Life Is a Dream

Whenever people tell me their dreams, I always say to them, "Dreams are illusions." However, illusory as they are, dreams are sometimes very interesting.

Early one morning before it was time to get up, I had a dream. A circle of light was flying toward me. Inside the circle was a familiar image of a woman. As she came near me, she folded her palms together and prostrated herself in front of me. She stood up and then seemed to wave goodbye. With that the light slowly disappeared. At this very moment, I heard the call to get up.

That dream, like others, was illusory, but I felt delighted with the dream even after I woke up.

The day before, I was told a commissioner had passed away and been cremated. I probably had that dream because I was thinking about her.

That commissioner was a good model for us, for she was very diligent. Although she was frail, she never missed the chance to volunteer at the Tzu Chi Hospital. She always encouraged herself with my words: "The human body can be compared to a car: to prolong the life of an old car, you have to use it frequently. If it is left parked, it will soon be junked as useless. So use the vehicle as much as you can while it is still usable." No matter how uncomfortable the old commissioner felt, she took every opportunity to come back and do volunteer work.

Once she went to a hospital for a physical examination. An x-ray examination revealed a black spot on her lung. The doctor cautioned her to be careful, but she did not heed the advice. Later on, another examination showed that the spot had grown. Only then did she go to the hospital for further diagnosis. It was discovered that she was in the terminal stage of lung cancer. The cancer cells had metastasized to her heart and led to pleural effusion. She was hospitalized immediately. Unfortunately, an exam for nurses was being held around that time, so many nurses were away. Our commissioner could not get immediate care, so another commissioner suggested she come back to Hualien Tzu Chi Hospital, which she did. When she arrived at the emergency room, the doctor knew right away that she had pleural effusion and drew 2000 cc of effusion from her body.

I was told that during her hospitalization, she was always smiling, even with an oxygen mask on. Never once did she show the slightest sign of being ill. When she was better, she walked around the hospital, enthusiastically encouraging patients and talking to them about Tzu Chi.

Two days before I left Hualien, where the hospital is located, to visit Tzu Chi branches around the island, I learned that a Tzu Chi commissioner had gone to the hospital, but I thought she went there to do volunteer work. When I found out that she was the patient, I decided to see her. She was very pleased and tidied herself up, for she wanted to look neat to show her respect.

When I saw her I was surprised for I did not expect it to be her. I said, "How come it's you?" She replied, "Master, I didn't let you know because I didn't want to make you worry."

"You don't look like a patient," I said.

"Right, so how can I be sick? Please don't worry."

"How are you feeling?"

"My heart and lungs are not very good. But it's nothing to worry about, Master."

Someone added, "She just had an operation yesterday. The doctor tapped 2000 cc of effusion from her body."

"You don't look as though you've just had an operation," I said. "You're really brave."

"I have to be brave. That's how I will beat the illness and recover."

She smiled widely and comforted me. "Master, my health has been like this. I'll be all right. I know you are short of volunteers. I'll try my best to battle this illness. Even if I lose, I'll come back with a new body soon to help you." She talked in a relaxed way, as if she were talking about somebody else's problems.

I told her, "I'm leaving and might not be able to see you again."

"Please don't come to see me again. I didn't want to let you know about my hospitalization in the first place."

After I returned from my tour around the island, I was very busy and didn't have time to see her. The next evening, a volunteer informed me that the commissioner had passed away. The following morning, I went to the mortuary to pay my respects. Her son was there. He seemed very calm. I said to him, "Your mother passed away peacefully, so don't be sad."

He replied, "She was very happy in the hospital because so many Tzu Chi sisters were there for her. Her happiness made me happy as well. I'll do as she said."

"What did your mother tell you to do?"

"She told me to fill in for her during her absence and join Tzu Chi."

"Good. With your reassurance, I'm sure she must have left calmly and will come back to Tzu Chi soon."

A volunteer told me that before she passed away, she shook hands with everyone and said thank you with a smile. Before she took her last breath, she asked her son, "Will you obey your mother?" Her son replied, "Of course, mom, I'll do as you told me." Then she said, "Go get some rest. I'm tired. I want to sleep now." He said, "All right." Then she closed her eyes and left us peacefully.

It is important to understand life and death. Although we do not know why we came into this world, we must be very clear when we leave the world about where we are going. That commissioner could be at ease with death because she harbored kindness, compassion and selflessness in her heart and she knew she would return to Tzu Chi. May she return soon.

Return to Save Living Beings

Breathing keeps one alive, so in a sense life exists in the span of a breath. The instant we stop breathing, life ends. It's as simple as that. Yet letting go of the last breath is not easy at all. Some terminally ill patients are reluctant to take their last breath and let go of life. They struggle feebly in a tug-of-war between life and death, hoping to keep breathing forever. How they torment themselves! They could be at ease and be released if they simply let go.

I remember during one of my visits to Tzu Chi Hospital, a volunteer informed me that a dying patient who was afflicted with nasopharyngeal cancer hoped to see me and become my disciple. I asked the volunteer to take me to the ICU to see him.

When we reached the ICU, a pretty young lady was waiting there. The volunteer introduced her as the wife of the patient. Together we went in to see him.

The wife gently held the head of her emaciated husband and whispered in his ear, "Look who's here. The Master has come to see you." They must have been a loving couple.

The patient forced his eyes to open. The look in his eyes seemed to say, "Master, at last I see you." Then he painstakingly turned his face toward me, and I stepped closer to him. "Your wish was to see me and to become my disciple," I said. "Now I'm here before you to offer you refuge. By taking refuge with the Buddha, his teachings, and with the assembly of monks and nuns, you become a disciple of these Three Treasures. You must remember to always think of the Buddha and mindfully chant the holy name of Amitabha Buddha. Remember to abide by the teachings of the Buddha. Do not be attached to worldly affairs; let go of them. You must always be committed to the Path of the Bodhisattvas in lives to come and resolve to be someone who can save others. Do you understand?"

A smile spread across his gaunt face. I knew he understood. He nodded, even though it was a strain for him to do so. "Remember to let go," I reminded him again. "You're lucky to have such a wonderful wife. She's been here with you day and night."

"Do you have any children?" I asked. His wife replied that they did not. "Then you can have no worries. Be a good disciple of the Three Treasures and keep in mind your commitment to save other people in the future. The body is nothing to cling to. The most important thing is to take good care of your mind. Let it be." He nodded again with great effort.

I sincerely prayed for his spiritual well-being. It is a pity that he was afflicted with such a fatal disease when he was only in his thirties and had to part with his dear wife. What excruciating torture his body and mind must have been going through.

The following day I went to the hospital for a meeting and ran into a young woman that I had seen the previous day outside the ICU. Since her father was also in the ICU, I asked her, "How is your father?" "He's much better now. But Master, the gentleman you visited yesterday passed away. He hadn't been able to move his hands, but after you left, he miraculously folded his palms together with great effort and chanted 'Amitabha' several times. He then left the world peacefully. His body was sent back to his home in

Taitung in eastern Taiwan yesterday." He had let go and was thus emancipated.

He truly was an obedient disciple of the Three Treasures. I had told him, "Let go, have no attachments, learn to behave like the Buddha, and vow to be a person capable of saving others." He observed my teachings, chanted the holy name of Amitabha, and passed away in peace. To learn to be a buddha means that in our everyday life, we have to learn to let go and let things be. Then we will be content and peaceful at the moment of death. That suffering patient had done so mindfully.

A Sincere Companion

If we have a clear and thorough understanding of life, we will be at peace and at ease no matter what situation we are in.

There was a young married woman who was in the terminal stage of cancer. She and her husband had visited many hospitals, but all the doctors told them there was nothing they could do to help. Each time their hopes were shattered. She was eventually admitted to the Hualien Tzu Chi Hospital. She became emotionally unstable, wailing, screaming, and raging at others each day to vent her anger and pain. The other patients in her ward couldn't stand it.

Despite her unreasonable behavior, her husband patiently tolerated and cared for her. They were truly a loving couple. They had been together since junior high school, and had never been parted until he went into the Army for two years of compulsory military service. One day when he was stationed on an offshore island of Taiwan, he received a letter from her. She wrote, "I have intestinal cancer. You'd better leave me and find a healthy girl."

He thought she was kidding, so he mischievously sent her three dried mosquitoes with a letter saying that she would be cured if she swallowed the mosquitoes with a glass of water. Never did he imagine that she was telling the truth. When he learned that she was not joking, he resolved to look after her until the end of her life. Not long after, they were married.

After the wedding, she suffered from constant relapses. They visited all the famous doctors. But they all told them, "This illness has no cure." Despite the discouraging news each time, they did not give up seeing doctors. The husband stayed with her all the way. Finally they came to the Hualien Tzu Chi Hospital. Our medical staff and volunteers took loving care not only of her body, but also her mind. Under such thorough care, she finally came to accept all that was happening to her and became calm again.

During her hospitalization, the husband and wife occasionally went on outings to the seashore or to the mountains. Sometimes on holidays our doctors and nurses joined them, because they hoped to help make the last stage of her rough life more joyful. One day her sister visited her and suggested that she make handicrafts to take her mind off the pain. The husband encouraged her as well and together they made a doll. Their first effort did not resemble a doll at all, but they did not give up. On Christmas Eve, two to three months later, the volunteers visited her and found her ward different. It was decorated with lovely handicrafts such as cloth dolls, flowers and birds. Her husband said, "These are the products of our love." All were beautifully made. Our volunteers encouraged her to make more.

The wife received much love from the volunteers. She realized that she should learn from their selfless giving and give of herself while she still could. She resolved to make handicrafts for Tzu Chi to sell at a charity bazaar. She tolerated her physical pain and concentrated on making handicrafts. With the help and care of our medical staff and volunteers, the young wife finally learned to live without regret. She said, "Now I know how to go on. My days in the hospital have been full of happiness." Moreover, she could accept the fact that she was dying and still be at ease because she finally knew how to make the best use of her life and walk towards death. Ridding herself of fear, she could open her heart and head toward the Path of the Bodhisattvas.

Mind alone creates everything. In the beginning when she found out she had cancer, her mind was unsettled and she was confused about how to carry on with her life. Such thinking made her life so miserable that she screamed and wailed. Once she had a clear understanding about life and death, she could face death peacefully and accept everything, even pain, with happiness. Thus, she could lead the rest of her life at ease and without regret.

The Brave Ones

Life is full of suffering. The worst suffering is sickness, for it tortures not only the body, but also the mind. Sickness may bring death, and this uncertainty makes one anxious and distressed, so that a one-day ordeal feels like a year. Physical illness is an undeniable part of life, but illness of the mind need not follow. If one can be optimistic and accept the illness, then mental anxiety will be alleviated. However, if one tries to deny the illness, mental suffering will compound one's physical suffering.

There was a Tzu Chi member who was afflicted with liver cancer, but his mind was free of anxiety. He remained optimistic and wished to return to Tzu Chi to live out the final stage of his life. In the Hualien Tzu Chi Hospital, we have a palliative ward named the Heart Lotus Ward, a cozy place where terminally ill patients can live and pass away peacefully under the care of doctors, nurses and volunteers. That Tzu Chi member was admitted to the Heart Lotus Ward.

When I went to see him, he calmly told me that he wanted to donate his body to medicine. For this reason, no matter how much pain he was in, he refused to receive electrotherapy or have an operation. He also told me that he wanted to leave the world with dignity. His manner was so casual and carefree, it seemed as if he were describing another patient. I was very touched. His peacefulness and ease of mind provided a positive influence for four other patients in his ward.

One of the patients in the ward was sitting in a chair chatting with another patient. An oxygen tube was attached to his nose. Unlike typical patients, he showed no signs of anxiety. I asked him, "Are you here to see a friend?" He pointed to an empty bed and said, "No, I'm one of the patients here."

"Master, I still do volunteer work," he told me. "This afternoon I'm going to take the patients of this ward downstairs to enjoy the sunshine and stroll in the garden." Although the end of his life was approaching, he had no fear and could courageously accept the fact. The last moments of his life were not squandered agonizing in bed; instead, they were used to serve other patients. He was truly a brave man.

Another brave old man, also with terminal cancer, was sitting in a wheelchair. When he saw me outside the ward, he first waved happily to me, then folded his palms together reverently as a sign of respect. Another old patient was chatting with someone in another ward. Although their days were numbered, they lived not in fear, but in joy.

"That old gentleman is very brave," a volunteer said to me. "He has grown orchids for years. Now that he's been hospitalized, he's moved more than a hundred pots here so that he can continue taking care of them. He said he would give them to the hospital to share their beauty with other patients." Upon hearing the word "orchid," he became very excited. Joyfully he said, "Yes, I grow orchids for people to see." Then he said to his son, "Go and show the Master our orchids. It takes special knowledge to grow them."

We walked to the garden where we found a hundred pots of orchids. The flowers made the garden very pretty. The patient's son introduced them to me one by one. "Master, this is New Year Orchid. This is Four Season Orchid. And this is…"

"This is Pure Heart Orchid, isn't it?" I said. He was surprised by my answer and asked, "Yes, it is, but how did you know?"

Actually, all orchids look the same to me. The only name I know is Pure Heart Orchid. "This kind of orchid smells nice when it blossoms."

He said, "Yes, Four Season Orchid is also fragrant when it blossoms." He took another pot in front of me and said, "Master, this is called Gold Lining Orchid. It used to be very expensive."

I said, "I heard that only two or three petals would cost a few million NT dollars."

"It's not that expensive now," he said.

There was a young man in his thirties with terminal cancer. He was also very brave. His face showed no signs of sickness; instead, he radiated confidence like a warrior in armor determined to win every battle. I encouraged him to fight on courageously.

"I will," he said. "I heard the story of Dr. Tu Shih-mien [the first superintendent of Tzu Chi Hospital, who died of liver cancer] and he inspired me." I observed that the doctor told Dr. Tu that he only had three months to live, but he lived for six more years after he wholeheartedly devoted himself to the construction and operation of our first hospital in eastern Taiwan. My reply seemed to give him confidence and comfort.

These patients and their family members in the Heart Lotus Ward contradicted the traditional dark, gloomy image of dying patients. Everyone's optimistic attitude made the Heart Lotus Ward a place filled with love, energy and joy.

Life exists in the span of a breath. You live as long as you breathe. The action of breathing has become so natural to us that we often are not aware of it. But some people painfully watch their breathing, uncertain if they will still be breathing the next hour, the next minute, or even the next second. How that uncertainty must torment them! But they can be released from anxiety if they only change their attitude and accept the fact that their breathing may cease at any moment.

We do not own our bodies, for we cannot even keep our bodies from the physical changes of growth, sickness and death. But we can control our minds and we have the right to use our bodies while we still possess them. So when we are in good health, we should take good care of our bodies and train our minds to accept anything that may come our way. When we fall ill, we should accept the fact bravely and not let fear or bewilderment pull us down. Since our time to use our bodies is limited, we must use them well to benefit society while we still can. We must use them until the last minute. When our time to part with this body comes, just let nature take its course.

Mr. Li

Learning to be like the Buddha means learning to be at ease with all matters, especially with our physical life. Birth, aging, illness and death are natural stages that life must go through. However, our mindset about these four phases varies. We often celebrate life, worry over aging, and fear death.

Since aging and death are inevitable, the best we can do to attain peace is to accept them. However, that is easier said than done. The path to buddhahood is never easy; aging and death are just two of the difficulties. We should face them with courage, and then peace will be with us.

In the Heart Lotus Ward, we had a good role model, Li Ho-cheng. He had been diagnosed with pancreatic cancer, and the doctor had told him that he had only three months to live. Unlike most people, Mr. Li was not defeated. Instead, he wanted to make the most of his remaining time to serve others. Even after his life came to an end, he wanted his body to be put to use for the benefit of society, so he decided to donate it to the anatomy class at the Tzu Chi medical college.

The first time I saw him, I was deeply impressed. He wore an easy smile, beaming with happiness. "You've been here two days. How do you feel?" "It feels like home, very warm," he replied. "I like it. I'm eating well and sleeping well, and I feel very relaxed." I told him that while he was here, he should exercise, take walks outside and chat with others. "Yes, and I can still do volunteer work; I'll visit with people and take other patients from my ward outside for a walk."

He really did take up work as a volunteer. Although he was physically too weak to render any service to other patients, he shared his experience in order to help them become stronger mentally. His easy, relaxed attitude brought an optimistic atmosphere to the palliative ward. The patients were so cheerful that they did not seem like people approaching the end of their lives. In Taiwan many people see talking about death as something ominous. However, Mr. Li held such a positive attitude about death that he could talk to a large group of visiting students about life and death calmly and peacefully. It was rare for anyone to have such an easy manner so near the end of life.

Not only was he brave, he was also diligent in doing good deeds and walking toward buddhahood. He knew that the Tzu Chi charity mission needed financial support, so he donated NT$1 million [US$30,300] and became an Honorary Board member of the Tzu Chi Foundation. More-over, he vowed to return to Tzu Chi again in many lives to come, and he asked me if he could be a disciple of mine. A few days later, I provided him with a certificate naming him a new Honorary Board member [this ceremony is usually held once a year, around Chinese New Year]. The ceremony meant a lot to him and he wanted to appear neat and solemn, so he asked the doctor to remove the nasogastric tube from his nose—a very painful process.

He was a true spiritual cultivator. He could face the end of his life calmly and with a smile. "It's not easy for you to have cultivated your mind to this degree," I said to him. "A real practitioner should be like you. Death is really nothing to be afraid of. It's a natural course in life."

If one can rid oneself of fear, then passing away is like falling asleep. Actually, everyone lives between life and death every day. After a day of hard work, we need to rest and sleep at night. Sometimes we dream. In that case, our souls and consciousness leave our bodies and float outside us.

Therefore, I always say, sleeping is a minor death. Everybody will experience one major death, a long sleep needed after a lifetime of work. Dying is similar to sleeping. When you die, your consciousness will also leave the body and float painlessly. After breathing stops completely, you must stay calm, know where you are heading, and guard your consciousness from being lured away by the outside environment. It is important to vow to return to the human world again to do good deeds. That vow will give you clear direction and help you remain calm. Your mental stability will be more easily attained if you constantly train your mind in your daily life.

Therefore, I said to him, "Have no fear. Just remember to guard your mind carefully when the last moment comes and hold on firmly to your vow of following me and saving people. There is nothing else to be afraid of." "I know," he said, "I'll do as you've told me." I continued, "It takes a lot of spiritual cultivation to talk about death and to accept everything fearlessly like you do." Although I was sad to part with him, I felt reassured as I saw his serene composure.

We come into this world, but one day our journey in this world will end and we will have to part from it. When that day comes, just let it be. Again, this is easier said than done. Many people still dread death, let alone dare to face it. Yet that is the lesson we have to learn: to train ourselves to conquer our fear and be at ease. The state of peace depends on our own efforts and the support of the people around us. In this sense, Mr. Li was very lucky, for he had a good wife who gave him consolation and accompanied him on the last journey of his life. In our lives, if we have no regrets, we can let go of this life peacefully and our wisdom will grow infinitely.

Approach the End with Joy

Day after day the sun rises and sets, waking up the world and then putting it to sleep. Year after year, it never fails to do so. As time flows, life seems to drift by. But a closer look reveals that in reality, different events are taking place at every second. Some people are born and some pass away. Some events happen and some end. Some things are formed and others are destroyed. Some give rise to joy and others bring sorrow. The world is indeed fascinating! In a single moment so much is happening. And nothing stays the same. Out of nothingness something rises, and then it disintegrates into nothingness again. The cycle of formation and extinction never ceases to cause problems or bring solutions.

How does something rise out of nothingness? Take material objects as an example. Many things we now have did not come into existence until someone invented and created them. Much time and effort were put into researching, inventing and experimenting. Those inventions have had various effects on the world. The same invention may have different consequences: sometimes beneficial to society, other times destructive. Take dynamite as an example. If it is used to build new roads or tunnel through mountains, it saves a great deal of labor and contributes greatly to transportation. But if it is used in the wrong hands, it will cause much suffering and death. Computers are beneficial if used to store huge amounts of information and improve communications. However, they can be destructive if used to perpetrate crimes or distribute harmful material.

Everything in the world rises and falls. Some things vanish so fast that they take all of us by surprise. This was the case of the passing away of a Tzu Chi commissioner.

It happened during the Moon Festival a few years ago. On that full moon night, many Tzu Chi people gathered together on the lawn outside the Abode of Still Thoughts to celebrate the occasion. They sang and danced joyfully. Of all the performances, an aboriginal dance won the most applause. Although everyone came from different places (some had never met before), they had fun and interacted like one big family.

The following day, they did volunteer work in the hospital. In the evening, the fine weather drew everyone out on the lawn again and the people chatted warmly. Many could not forget the aboriginal dancing performed the previous day. A commissioner from Taitung remarked that they had practiced several days for the performance and that the dance was simple if one knew the steps. Everyone asked her to demonstrate.

So she stood up to show them. But right after she said, "Come on, let's dance together," she collapsed to the ground. Everyone was dumbfounded for a few seconds before they realized that something was wrong and rushed her to the Tzu Chi Hospital. On the way, her eyes were still open and she reassured everyone that she was fine. But with that said, she closed her eyes again and was gone.

How fleeting life can be! A few minutes before, she had been full of life, happy and serene. Then in an instant she fainted and was on her way to the hospital. Even though she knew she was dying, she was still at ease, clear-headed and ready to leave the world. Her mind was crystal clear, without any attachments. Impermanent as it was, her life was a good one for she could pass away peacefully.

Her husband said the times that his wife participated in Tzu Chi activities were the happiest times in her life. She liked them so much. Whenever it was her turn to volunteer at Tzu Chi Hospital, she would get very excited, like a little schoolgirl going on an outing. She was a Tzu Chi volunteer to the last minute of her life.

After the funeral, her husband said that he was grateful to all Tzu Chi members for their help and care. He would take up whatever Tzu Chi work his wife had not finished. Both husband and wife really had the hearts of bodhisattvas, full of gratitude.

One of the purposes of spiritual cultivation is to learn to live so well that we can pass away without sickness, struggle, fear, attachment, or confusion. I'm so glad that she lived such a life! Life is short, so we have to make good use of our time and be mindful in everything that we do.

Set a Good Example

In the Heart Lotus Ward, there was a patient who was close to ninety years old. She had been a Tzu Chi member for over three decades. Although she passed away, her altruistic deeds and serene attitude in facing death remain good examples for others to follow.

One of her final wishes was to see me before she passed away. When she saw me, my good old disciple greeted me with neither grief nor fear over death, but with a brilliant smile instead—very untypical for a dying person. She was one of my earliest followers when I started the Tzu Chi Foundation over thirty years ago. Those three decades were marked with much hardship. I held her wrinkled hand in mine and asked her, "Do you remember how long you have been with me?" "Maybe more than thirty years," she said. "To be exact, it's been thirty-three years," I reminded her. "And you have done a lot of good deeds in that time." She humbly replied that she had not done much, for she was not a smart person.

I told her not to feel that way, because she was in truth very wise. It was she and other senior commissioners who first carried out my call to help people. In the beginning we had nothing, but they began by saving fifty cents [US$0.02] each day and they even mustered up the courage to ask people in the market to do the same. And even at that very moment she was still helping me. My words made her smile. She asked her daughter to get something for me and refused to tell me what it was. She said mysteriously, "You'll see."

Her daughter came back with a jewelry box in her hand. I said to her, "I know what it is." I opened the box and teased her, "You're good at hiding your savings, aren't you? What a large gold ring! What is it for?" She said that she had bought the ring with the money she had saved over the years, and it was to help me build hospitals. "I'll do as you wish," I promised. "Are you at peace? Never forget to return to the world and follow me closely in helping people. You must sincerely vow to do so." She reached out and held my hand. I told her that she should remember to always hold my hand firmly like she was doing. Yet she had doubts that she would meet me again. I told her not to worry, for she would defi-nitely return if her vow to follow me was firm and her mind crystal clear and free of attachments. She was delighted and thanked me happily.

Although she knew she was dying, she smiled heartily without a tinge of sorrow. She passed away peacefully.

Her serene composure seemed to hint that her life had been one without worry, but that was not so. She had had her share of difficulties, but she could be at peace and always smiling because of her broad-mindedness. She often reminded other Tzu Chi people to abide by my teachings by always thinking from another's point of view and by being more accommodating.

Indeed, she was our role model. People often like to find fault and criticize others. But this old bodhisattva was lenient with everyone, including her own relatives and other Tzu Chi members. Never in her life did she hold a grudge against others.

She was a contented person, always thankful for all that she had. I frequently praised her for being a good disciple of the Buddha, which she said was what all Buddhists

should be. She told me, "Tzu Chi people are spiritual culti-
vators, so we have to be broad-minded. We speak for others
to listen and act for others to see." Her simple words had
profound meaning: Tzu Chi people should set good examples for others to follow.

Although I was sad over her departure, I was also happy
for her, for she had lived a long life without regret. In her life,
she had the chance to hear and practice the Buddha's teachings. Even though she had suffered from physical illness, she
did not let it worry her or create an illness of the mind. So let
us just pray for her.

Another commissioner was also hospitalized. But unlike
the ninety-year-old commissioner, she was not at ease with
impending death. Seeing her struggling painfully on the
threshold between life and death, I sincerely hoped that she
would either get well soon or leave the world and her tor-
turous sickness.

Before she passed away, I went to the ICU to see her. She
looked peaceful. I said to her, "I know you want to hear me
say, 'Remember to come back quickly.' Now is the time for
you to leave this world. Remember to go peacefully and
come back soon. You've chosen Tzu Chi as the path you want
to take. You're already walking on it, so don't be distracted
by worldly affairs and go astray. Return to the human world
again and concentrate on walking the path of Tzu Chi." Her
daughter also told her not to worry because she would take
up her unfinished work in Tzu Chi.

No one can predict the length of life. The most important
thing is to know the true nature of this body. Your body is a
mere combination of the four elements of earth, water, fire

and air. It is comparable to an automobile: when the four elements are in balance, a car will run well, and your body will stay fit. But if they are not in balance, the car will break down, and you will be taken ill. However if you insist on driving a run-down car on a rough, winding road, you are rashly putting yourself in danger. The wise decision is to get rid of that car and find a new, powerful one to embark on the journey of a new life.

I think her daughter's reassurance was the best consolation she needed to give up that broken car, leave the rough road of this life and change to a powerful new car.

In ordinary times, we have to train ourselves to sit calmly in the driver's seat and accept whatever condition the car might be in. When it is time to get out of the car, we can do so with ease. We should not be confused by the road ahead of us or restrained by the condition of the car. Let go when it is time to. Life is a mystery. It can be tenacious if the karma we have to experience in this life is not finished. It can be fragile and terminate instantly if our destiny for this life ends. Then we will drift where our karma takes us.

Life exists in the span of a breath. Without the motions of inhaling and exhaling, we would not be alive. But breathing is not always easy. Life, like many other things, is beyond our control. What we can control is our minds. We can emulate the Buddha in facing calmly whatever may come to us. Take a look at life. When it ends, there is nothing we can take with us except karma. So why compete for more, and why limit our love to a few? Wise people know that they should love all beings under the sky equally; this is called "enlightened love." This enlightened love leads to the Path of the Bodhisattvas. Without a doubt my two disciples both harbored enlightened love, so they will return to the world again to redeem all beings from their sufferings.